A Guide

TO THE

World
Wide
Web

Lory Hawkes, Ph.D.

 Prentice Hall, Upper Saddle River, New Jersey 07458

Library of Congress Cataloging-in-Publication Data

Hawkes, Lory
    A guide to the World Wide Web / Lory Hawkes.
        p.   cm.
    Includes index.
    ISBN 0-13-273509-1
        1. World Wide Web (Information retrieval system)   2. Netscape.
    3. Microsoft Internet Explorer.   I. Title.
    TK5105.888.H385   1998
    004.67'8—dc21   98-28724
                                                                          CIP

Editor in chief: *Charlyce Jones-Owen*
Executive editor: *Leah Jewell*
Assistant editor: *Patricia Castiglione*
Managing editor: *Bonnie Biller*
Production liaison: *Fran Russello*
Editorial/production supervision: *Publisher's Studio*
Prepress and manufacturing buyer: *Mary Ann Gloriande*
Cover director: *Jayne Conte*
Cover designer: *Kiwi Design*
Cover image illustrator: *Lori Osiecki*
Illustrator: *Stratford Publishing Services*
Copy editor: *Leslie Connor*
Marketing manager: *Rob Mejia*

This book was set in 10 point Palatino by Stratford Publishing
Services and was printed and bound by Courier Companies, Inc.
The cover was printed by Phoenix Color Corp.

 © 1999 by Prentice-Hall, Inc.
Simon & Schuster/A Viacom Company
Upper Saddle River, New Jersey 07458

Printed in the United States of America
10   9   8   7   6   5   4   3   2   1

ISBN   0-13-273509-1

Prentice-Hall International (UK) Limited, *London*
Prentice-Hall of Australia Pty. Limited, *Sydney*
Prentice-Hall of Canada Inc., *Toronto*
Prentice-Hall Hispanoamericana, S.A., *Mexico*
Prentice-Hall of India Private Limited, *New Delhi*
Prentice-Hall of Japan, Inc., *Tokyo*
Simon & Schuster Asia Pte. Ltd., *Singapore*
Editora Prentice-Hall do Brasil, Ltda., *Rio de Janeiro*

To my husband, Bob,
for his support, his concern,
and his humor

Contents

CHAPTER TWO   HYPERTEXT LORE   11

CHAPTER THREE   WEB PROFILE   24

CHAPTER NINE   ADVANCED AUTHORING   137

CHAPTER 10   DREAMSCAPES & EXPERIMENTS   158

List of Shortlists

Templates

Preface

The World Wide Web (WWW) is an anomaly. A unique, freeform virtual society brought about by technological innovation and stimulated by the resurgence of self-directed investigation, the Web challenges new explorers to find their way through its morass of sites by mastering software-driven graphical browsers.

With its nontechnical explanations about the Internet and the Web, *A Guide to the World Wide Web* will help build your confidence to venture through the Web's chaos of information with the two latest graphical browsers, Netscape Navigator 4.0 and Internet Explorer 4.0. Different from other WWW texts, this book uses supporting Web pages at a companion Web site (http://homepages. waymark.net/~hawkes/guide/guidewww.html) and encourages Web page authorship to increase your ability to gain information, synthesize it, and then reformulate it into your own Web page design. *A Guide to the World Wide Web* includes:

- A series of supporting Web pages to extend and reinforce the chapters of the book.
- A quick trip to find out what is new and valued on the Web.
- A thoughtful orientation to hypertext theory, the guiding principle of Web architecture and digital exchanges.
- An examination of Web demographics to build an appreciation of its dynamic history and an understanding of its users as the audience for your Web pages.
- A multitude of shortlists to help you learn your way around the Web and build confidence to explore on your own.
- Savvy tips on how to write for the Web as well as individual and collaborative writing assignments.

- Clear and careful explanations to make your searches more productive with a focused research question, a carefully selected search engine, a well-crafted query statement, and a handy discovery journal to record your findings.
- Documentation advice and examples of citing electronic sources in both the Modern Language Association style and the American Psychological Association style.
- Classroom-tested guidelines and helpful HTML templates for creating and refining Web pages.
- Thoughtful advisories about the risks of communication on the Web and about societal issues related to virtual environments.

Acknowledgments

To pay tribute to Marshall McLuhan and Bruce R. Powers, each chapter begins with an excerpt from their last collaborative work, *The Global Village.* Published a decade ago, the book refines McLuhan's philosophy of virtual space and electronic communication. Although the work studies television, the findings are also valid for the digital village of the World Wide Web. McLuhan and Powers describe the electronic medium as a fusion of the physical world and a virtual world, which suspends humans in a state of heightened awareness. In their groundbreaking study, the authors predict that the rapid transfer of information and unlimited opportunity to exchange ideas will dramatically affect the future. Now, from the future, judge the relevance of these predictions by reading their words.

My thanks goes to my children Matt, Chris, Greg, and Leslie for their suggestions and to my mother for her encouragement. A special thanks goes to Gwen Allison, whose insightful comments refined the information in the book, as well as to these colleagues who reviewed this book: Valeria Balester, Texas A & M University; Maria Dinchak, Glendale Community College; Will Hochman, University of Southern Colorado; Marcia Peoples Malio, University of Delaware; Margaret-Rose Marek, Texas Christian University; and Ted McFerrin, Collin County Community College. My appreciation goes to the professionals at Prentice-Hall, Leah Jewell, Kara Hado, and Triscia Liscio, who all helped to make this book a reality.

CHAPTER ONE
Quick Trip

Travel Strategy
Award Winners
Emerging Genres

At electronic speeds all forms are pushed to the limit of their potential: on the telephone (or on the air) it is not the message that travels at electronic speed. What actually occurs is that the sender is sent, minus a body, and all the old relationships of speaker and audience tend to be erased.

THE GLOBAL VILLAGE

TRAVEL STRATEGY

The **World Wide Web** is a vibrant online community of computer users with diverse interests and opinions. An unusual space, the Web can be intimidating to new travelers. However, this quick "siteseeing" trip will orient you to the Web, building your confidence and your savvy about **cyberspace**— a vast, collaborative, virtual area accessible through interconnected computers. Just as travel to unusual places brings us into contact with different cultures and customs, successful navigation of the boundless Information Superhighway depends on your readiness to find and assimilate information

Order of occurrence	→ Shortlist 0. Descriptive Category of Web Sites
Web Site Name	→ Guide to WWW Companion Web Site
URL	→ http://homepages.waymark.net/~hawkes/index.htm

FIGURE 1.1 *Shortlist Example*

while abiding by the customs of the virtual culture. One of the surest ways to begin to learn about the Web is to take this brief, focused trip to find out how to travel, to see what the Web community values as its award-winning sites, and to experience the diversity of creative works emerging as Web-based **genres**—discernible types of content that have distinguishing characteristics like an interactive novel or an online discussion.

Just as unique as virtual space is your steering device, the mouse, and the magical looking glass that is your browser's window which allows you to pass through virtual space into the dynamic Web. Since time is of the essence, we'll help you devise a travel strategy by preselecting relevant and useful Web sites, discussing their purposes or special attributes, and listing their Web addresses, known as **uniform resource locators (URLs),** and site names in Shortlists (Figure 1.1) as part of every chapter. (Note that some URLs may have changed due to the tendency of Web developers to constantly improve their sites.)

Tour Options

If you are a novice to Web travel, you should take the full scenic tour by reading this book's discussions to understand the background of individual sites, what they represent, and why they are important to see. In this way, you will be oriented to their purpose, nature, and distinguishing features before you visit them as Shortlist sites. If you are a frequent Web traveler, you may skim discussions of sites you know well, but stop and linger at the new array of sites in the Shortlists to learn about their content as well as their technique of presenting information in a virtual space. However, if you are an experienced Web traveler, you may elect to use the Shortlists as an expedient discovery route to find new sites or to reorient yourself to the dramatically changing landscape of the Web.

To acclimate you to the new vocabulary of virtual culture, a Web Lingo section at the end of each chapter provides a summary of the key terms highlighted in boldface throughout the chapters, while the Glossary at the end of the book defines these terms. Each chapter's Web Itinerary supplies meaningful exercises to build your personal ability to navigate and evaluate what you have found, and Project Assignments suggest collaborative ventures to share your experiences with others. Although beginning chapters include Travel Tips to help novice users anticipate how to use the browser as a tool in their tour, later chapters eliminate these tips because by then you will feel like an experienced traveler and be able to accomplish most tasks relying on your own fact-finding intuition. In addition, specially developed Web pages in a companion site reinforce the content of the chapters by further demonstrating a technique, providing effortless access to important knowledge archives, furnishing extended explanations, and supplying handy models for Web page design, which occurs in the concluding chapters. Figure 1.2 shows the supporting Web page for this chapter displayed in the Netscape 4.0 browser.

Charting a Landmark

If you are new to the Web, determining whether a site is a memorable one and keeping track of its location can be a chore. Fortunately, guided by the following quick test for the sufficiency, quality, and usefulness of a site's

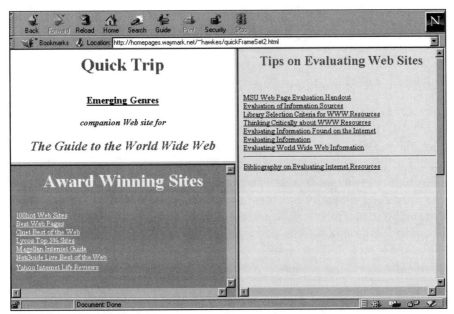

FIGURE 1.2 *Quick Trip Supporting Web Page*

content, your instincts can help you decide whether to investigate the details of a site, come back later to explore it, or move on somewhere else.

- Does the site have a comprehensive collection of information?
- Is the site's content logically organized in a clear and useful system?
- Are facts accurate—as far as you can judge?
- Do summaries of historical events, characterizations of well-known people, and descriptive details about places seem to be treated with respect?
- Does the site present a new topic or provide a unique treatment of an old topic?
- Is there visual appeal that invites easy, self-directed exploration?
- Does the site have *timeliness*, serving as a forum for a current crisis, a commonly held concern, or a staging ground for an Internet initiative?
- Does the site draw you into the content and make you eager to discover all the information it holds?
- Does the site provide **bookmarks** (electronic pointers to other Web site locations) to encourage further exploration of the subject matter?
- Does the site contain a bibliography of works that seem to be relevant, respected, and recent?

As a result of increased publishing of original work and of republishing of formerly printed work, researchers are in the process of formulating criteria for site evaluations to guide Web users (Shortlist 1). Leading the way are university libraries.

Uncovering Document Information

Yet another way to make a speedy evaluation of a site is to view information about the document's origin and file structure. Every Web site consists of files that structure its data. This structure becomes a history of the site and a map to the organization of the site's files. For example, you can find out the author, the date of creation, and under what filenames supporting documents and clarifying graphic files are stored. Figure 1.3 shows the document information for the home page of Netscape. To make the browser show document information, you have to use menu commands located at the top of the browser and then select an option from that menu command submenu. The command sequences for both browsers are shown in Figure 1.3 on page 6.

SHORTLIST 1
Evaluating Web Sites

Bibliography on Evaluating Internet Resources
http://refserver.lib.vt.edu/libinst/critTHINK.HTM

Britannica Information Guide (subscription required)
http://www.ebig.com/Help22.html

Cornell Univ. Library's How to Critically Analyze Information Sources
http://www.library.cornell.edu/okwref/research/skill26.htm

Evaluating Internet Resources: A Checklist
http://infopeople.berkeley.edu:8080/bkmk/select.html

Evaluating Information Sources
http://www.udmercy.edu/htmls/academics/library/evaluate.html

Evaluating Information Found on the Internet
http://milton.mse.jhu:8001/research/education/net.html

Evaluating World Wide Web Information
http://thorplus.lib.purdue.edu/library_info/instruction/gs175/3gs175/evaluation.html

Evaluation of Information Sources
http://www.vuw.ac.nz/~agsmith/evaln/index.htm

Internet Source Validation Project
http://www.stemnet.nf.ca/curriculum/vladate.html

Library Selection Criteria for WWW Resources
http:/wwwb.pilot.infi.net/~carolyn/criteria.html

Thinking Critically about WWW Resources
http://www.library.ucla.edu/libraries/college/instruct/critical.htm

Univ. of Wisconsin 10C's for Evaluating Internet Resources
http://www.uwec.edu/admin/library/10cs.html

AWARD WINNERS

As a virtual community, the World Wide Web recognizes leadership, talent, and technical achievement with awards. Sites proudly carry an award emblem in a conspicuous location on their beginning page called a **home page**, which is the first page of a Web site. These outstanding sites are benchmarks by which other sites can be measured. As the best examples of sites, they also are

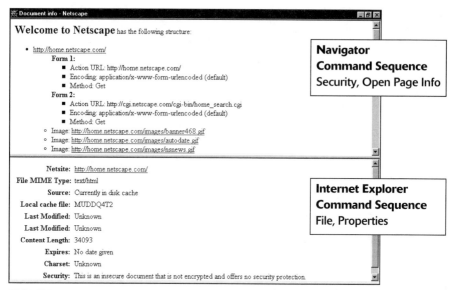

FIGURE 1.3 *Viewing Document Information*

models of superior expressive quality and technological accomplishment. A few of the sites are so remarkable that they display multiple awards.

Whether the award comes from the Lycos Search Engine as the Top 5% of all Web sites or belongs to C/net that names the Best of the Web, site owners relish the honor and the increased traffic generated by the designation. Moreover, since award-winning sites often complement an arrangement of text with artful images, these sites provide new users with a frame of reference for judging other sites during their travels and a standard for analyzing their own sites. Chiefly, there are two kinds of awards: a ranking and a favorable review. Rankings can be a superlative adjective to describe the site like Netscape's "coolest site of the day," or a symbol like the five stars NetGuide Live uses to indicate superior accomplishment. Rankings are the result of a process. A common practice encourages nominations from Web users. Next, a panel of experts judge nominated sites for content, appearance, operation, and coherence. Finally, the winning sites garnering a high score or a consensus of favorable responses are awarded the superior rank.

As a contrast, the worst sites also receive recognition. These sites may be the first Web pages of new users or illogical attempts to communicate information; some of these pages even belong to corporations that fail to provide functional access to product information. Unlike the rankings for the best sites, the worst sites may be part of an annotated list by an individual who maintains a personal Web page devoted to finding loser sites. Since the designation is more of an embarrassment, the worst Web site owner tends to quickly improve the site or dismantle it.

In addition to ranking sites, Web guides like NetGuide, Magellan, and Yahoo write short, sometimes pointed analyses of sites in Web-published reviews. Offering reviews that appeal to a cross section of users, Magellan Internet Guide and Lycos Top 5% Sites generally provide balanced views of sites. Reviews help new users focus early exploration on the best sites, and they also give new users a gauge to measure sites they find on their own. Shortlist 2 provides the URLs to ranking sites and review sites.

SHORTLIST 2
Site Ranking and Guides

100hot Web Sites
http://www.100hot.com

Best Web Pages
http://www.baylor.edu/~Lisa_Ezra/BESTweb.htm

C|net Best of the Web
http://www.cnet.com/Content/Reviews/Bestofweb

Lycos Top 5% Sites
http://point.lycos.com

Magellan Internet Guide
http://www.mckinley.com

NetGuide Live Best of the Web
http://www.netguide.com

Yahoo Internet Life Reviews
http://www.zdnet.com/yil

EMERGING GENRES

As the Web becomes a hub for experiments in publishing genres, or types of creative work, new artforms are emerging to intrigue and inspire a growing reading audience. Extending itself beyond its original purpose as an **index**, or a comprehensive topical list of Web sites, Yahoo continues to be an authority on Web site innovation as it seeks out new creative forms and groups them into easily explored categories. Although Yahoo has a user-friendly look with a search box inviting user-defined keywords, it also provides an index of alphabetically arranged categories called a **knowledge tree** that follows its search box.

Figure 1.4 illustrates the appearance of the knowledge tree for the portion of Yahoo that holds the Arts:Humanities:Literature:Genres groupings. Although the topical areas within this grouping change in response to new, creative works, the knowledge tree is a convenient stop to experience the potential of the Web as it transforms, adapts, and reinvents expressive works.

A few new genres play with language and visual appearance to create a mood. Noted in Shortlist 3, ToadHead experiments with the power of suggestion through text and graphics. Essays or poetry appear against a background of artwork so that the two blend together. Cracks in the Web is a site with spine-tingling episodes of an interactive novel richly illustrated and easy to navigate. Awarded Netscape's Cool Site of the Day and recognized as one of the Lycos Top 5%, you may change the focus of the story by selecting a character's picture from a gallery of principal characters.

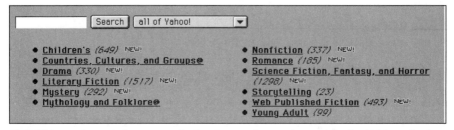

FIGURE 1.4 *Genre Subcategory of Yahoo. Text and artwork copyright © 1998 by Yahoo! Inc. All rights reserved. YAHOO! and the YAHOO! logo are trademarks of YAHOO! Inc.*

SHORTLIST 3
New Genres

Architects of the Web
http://www.architectsoftheweb.com

Cracks in the Web
http://www.directnet.com/~gmorris/title.html

Engines for Education Hyperbook
http://www.ils.nwu.edu/~e_for_e/

SitCom 2000
http://www.sitcom2000.com/

ToadHead
http://www.spies.com/ToadHead/index.choices.html

Through the Looking Glass

The following exercises allow you to explore and draw conclusions about what you see; in essence, you get to be the expert.

WEB LINGO

bookmarks	knowledge tree
cyberspace	uniform resource locator (URL)
genre	World Wide Web
home page	

TRAVEL TIP: USING THE URL IN THE BROWSER

1. In order to specify where you want to travel, you must find the location box (Netscape browser) or the Netsite box (Internet Explorer) of your browser.
2. Use your mouse pointer to click at the leftmost edge of the box. The mouse pointer will change to an I-beam.
3. Carefully type in the URL in the browser box making sure that all capitalization and punctuation is correct.

http://www.whitehouse.gov

4. Although browsers vary, usually striking the enter key after you have typed in the URL will start the browser looking for the Web site.

WEB ITINERARY

1. Travel to the New Genres in Yahoo by typing in the Web site address in the browser or using the companion Web page for this chapter. Write down the subcategories of fiction.
2. Travel to the sites that offer evaluation advice. Print out what you think is the best advice.

3. Appoint yourself as an expert. Explore the best sites of the Web. Select one site that you consider to be the best. Write a paragraph to tell why.

PROJECT ASSIGNMENT

Planning: Separate into groups.

Brainstorm about the things that freshmen need to know to survive their first semester in your college or university. Prepare a knowledge tree with broad categories that divide the information into major sections. Take each major section and divide it into subcategories.

Ranking: When you have finished, compare your knowledge tree to those of the other groups. Establish criteria to judge content and effective arrangement of information. Apply this criteria to all the knowledge trees. Rank all of the knowledge trees from first to last. Display the best of the knowledge trees.

In-Class Writing: Write an award notice to the winning group in which you:

1. Describe their accomplishment.
2. Note the criteria they met or exceeded.
3. Describe any flaws that might need work.

If you are in the winning group, write a consolation notice to the group with the lowest ranking. After you have closely studied their knowledge tree:

1. Praise their participation.
2. Identify the criteria that was used.
3. Discuss the strengths and weaknesses of their entry.

CHAPTER TWO

Hypertext Lore

| Conceptual Machine
| Innovative Refinements
| Theory

> *Electronic man wears his brain outside his skull and his nervous system on top of his skin . . . He is like an exposed spider squatting in a thrumming web, resonanting with all other webs.*
>
> THE GLOBAL VILLAGE

CONCEPTUAL MACHINE

Appearing in the September 1945 issue of *Life* magazine, Vannevar Bush's visionary essay about a revolutionary machine to help humankind was a stark contrast to the chilling photographs of the charred remains at Hiroshima. As President Franklin D. Roosevelt's Science Advisor, Vannevar Bush (Figure 2.1) was an influential man in the government and a respected

FIGURE 2.1 *Vannevar Bush, Science Advisor to President Franklin D. Roosevelt. Reprinted, by permission, from the MIT Museum and Archive.*

scientist who had originally published his essay, "As We May Think," in *The Atlantic Monthly*. The *Life* article teased readers with a longer title: "As We May Think: A top U.S. scientist foresees a possible future world in which man-made machines will start to think." The text of the essay contained illustrations to heighten readers' interest and help them visualize the theoretical machine that Bush promised would allow scientists and citizens alike to keep up with scientific research.

Bush's conceptual machine, the **Memex,** was an ordinary office desk which housed an array of pulleys and levers to fetch microcards and subsequently mount the cards for viewing on twin panels. Although file cabinets were the primary storage devices, this electromechanical retrieval system worked in tandem with the user to locate and display information on demand. Foreshadowing electronic search engines now commonplace on the Web, the Memex contained an immense data bank of microcards holding miniaturized reports, articles, and essays that could be made readable by means of the TV-like panels.

Not only did Bush's machine offer nonsequential access to cards stored in the desk, the operating characteristics of the Memex were similar to a **browser**, which is a software-enabled viewing screen for text and graphics on Web pages. As the Memex did, the browser enables the user to annotate any displayed document. Observing that adding a personal note on the reading material would be a way to synthesize the material by marking its significance or by adding a suddenly triggered thought, Dr. Bush proposed a revolutionary concept of coauthorship between the original author and the user. In essence, he believed that too much information brought about too little use of it. Information became valuable only if it could be accessed, assimilated, and applied to meet a user's needs. In other words, Bush wanted information to be accessible, usable, and shareable.

In the late summer of 1945, Vannevar Bush envisioned an answer to the outgrowth of escalating technological publishing we call information overload. With his machine, he offered to scientists and laypeople the potential for accessing unlimited knowledge and the unique ability to examine documents in any order that suited the machine user to mark on them.

Fifty years later, Bush's theoretical machine is still an inspiration for the virtual society of the World Wide Web. In fact, when MIT celebrated the fiftieth Anniversary of the Memex, Ian Adelman, with the assistance of Paul Kahn, developed an animation of the Memex to show its simple design and remarkable potential (Figure 2.2). Paul Kahn, President of Dynamic Diagrams, retains the rights to the animation and has granted permission to link this animation to the companion Web site.

Since hypertext theory is the organizing principle governing the World Wide Web and guiding its future development, Bush's essay and his machine are rightfully the starting point of our discussion of the Web's history and the focus of the resources listed in Shortlist 4. However, innovative refinements by other visionaries helped shape the Web and influenced the development of Web browsers.

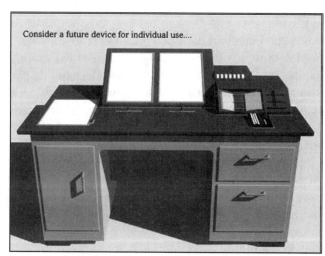

FIGURE 2.2
Commemorative animation of the Memex. Reprinted, by permission, from Dynamic Diagrams.

SHORTLIST 4
Memex Resource

"As We May Think"
http://www.isg.sfu.ca/~duchier/misc/vbush

Memex
http://eies.njit.edu/~333/review/memex.1.html

Memex (Electronic Labyrinth)
http://jefferson.village.virginia.edu/elab/hfl0051.html

Memex Animation
http://www.dynamicdiagrams.com:80/design/memex/model.htm

Vannevar Bush and the Memex (Slide Show)
http://libwww.stfx.ca/hypermedia/presentations/session1/sed010.html

---

INNOVATIVE REFINEMENTS

Window Environment

Bush's essay caused a minor stir when it was published, but it was almost twenty years before reaction to his theoretical machine resulted in any technological innovation. One of the first software applications developed by programmers who had read Bush's essay was the **oN Line System (NLS)** spearheaded by Douglas Engelbart for the Augmented Human Intellect Research Center in 1968. Inspired by his theoretical extension of Bush's Memex in his 1963 essay "A Conceptual Framework for the Augmentation of Man's Intellect," Engelbart designed NLS as a large **database**, an array of fields that hold data which can be arranged and recalled through programming statements. This NLS was programmed to select and display text in multiple windows on the monitor. To distinguish the text from the programming statements, angle brackets enclosed the alphanumerical codes, which categorized the information. Five windows performed different tasks which enabled the morass of information to be scanned by a computer and organized for logical responses to user requests for information (Conklin 22). Although text based, Engelbart's system was the beginning of the **graphical user interface (GUI)**, which represents functions and options with graphical characters to increase user-friendly operation and conceal complex programming statements. The interface was used in conjunction with a new input device, the mouse ("Conceptual Beginnings").

Large Scale Document Retrieval

Adapting Bush's dream machine to his own purpose, programmer Ted Nelson foresaw an expansive global network of literary works that could be indexed and retrieved. For the first time, he made the distinction that a literary work could be a hypertext document that had links to other documents or held "windowing text" (Conklin 23). Not only was Nelson the originator of the terms *hypertext* and *hypermedia* ("Hypertext Collaboration"), he was also an early soothsayer about the new form of public access to digital libraries. In his system called a **docuverse** (Figure 2.3), literary holdings could be checked out electronically, and a tracking system would audit activity to ensure proper payment of fees for copyrighted material. To effectively deal with the diversity of computer hardware or the incompatibility of operating systems that might hamper the exchange of information, he adopted **UNIX** as the operating system. Like Bush, Nelson wanted his literary archive to be available to the public. Moreover, his concept of windowing text correctly anticipated current Web page design that permits segmentation of a Web page into windows, or frames, which have separate content.

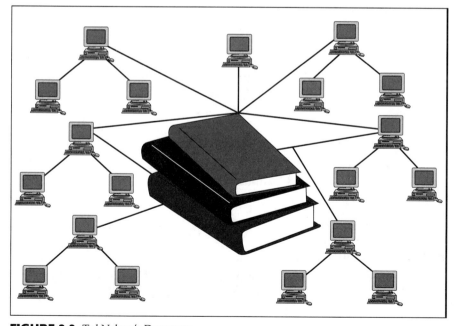

FIGURE 2.3 *Ted Nelson's Docuverse*

Links and Frames

Quick to spot the scholarly potential of hypertext, Randall Trigg's dissertation for the University of Maryland in 1983 anticipated the shift from paper-based publishing to electronic publishing, the use of computerized searching to find obscure works, the coauthoring of documents for online journals, and the concept of a path, by which the hypertext system provides an avenue of travel inviting the user to follow as link after link is displayed (Conklin 24). His Textnet system organized files into a hierarchy or knowledge tree of topics that in turn linked to separate text files (Conklin 24). Coming on the heels of Textnet in 1981, the **Knowledge Management System (KMS)** by Donald McCracken and Robert Akscyn appeared as a series of frames. Each KMS frame had a title followed by numbered selections offering links to additional information. A navigation bar at the bottom of the frame contained simple word commands for *help, back, next,* and *return* as well as text-changing commands like *edit* and *comment.*

Ben Schneiderman intended **Hyperties (Hyper The Interactive Encyclopedia System)** to be an informational model for the University of Maryland, and later developed it for IBM. As a commercial application it incorporated **hot spots**, distinguished from normal text as blue-colored words or phrases. When a user pressed the hot spot on a touch-sensitive screen, the display jumped to a corresponding article described by the hot spot. **Symbolics Document Examiner** could alter screen displays to show a different topic and return quickly to the previous screen with a system of **bookmarks,** while Xerox PARC's **NoteCards** provided a flexible link structure to make hot spots of selected text perform preprogrammed commands. Each of the main Note-Card functions—text building, command definition, and links—appeared on the background of a notecard. The notecard was the GUI interface and a visual metaphor for the program itself. Closing out the early years of hypertext innovation, Brown University's **Intermedia** project pioneered the concept of a web of files linked to another web and introduced a means to represent a virtual landscape as a map of links (Conklin 26–29). In Shortlist 5, hypertext timelines reveal the rapid and stunning refinement of Bush's theory.

Interface and Database

The World Wide Web evolved from a corporate initiative to make research more available to scientists at Centre Européen pour la Récherche Nucleaire (CERN), a physics research facility in Switzerland. It had a database of hypertext documents delivered by a GUI browser. Similar to the display panels on

---

SHORTLIST 5
Hypertext Timelines

Electronic Labyrinth's Hypertext Timeline (367-1995)
http://jefferson.village.virginia.edu/elab/hf0267.html

Histories of the Internet and the WWW
http://www.utm.edu/~aaff/history.htm

Hypermedia Timeline
http://geosci.uchicago.edu/guide/guide.app.a.html
http://www.hcc.hawaii.edu/guide/www.guide.app.a.html
http://www.iu.net/guide/guide.14.html

Hypertext History
http://ei.cs.vt.edu/~cs5604/U-HT/subsection3_2_1.html

Bush's machine which made the miniature documents visible, the browser translated virtual text and pictures into visible text and pictures. However, the Web went beyond the basic purpose of joining together CERN scientists and became an open public community which offered the opportunity for self-publishing. In 1988, CERN scientists and their colleagues in the Amsterdam Mathematics Center began exchanging electronic correspondence (Reddick and King 54). Tim Berners-Lee, the Father of the Web, developed the World Wide Web program so that users could get "raw information" and make annotations to it without having to use programming statements or deal with more technical designators like URLs (Interview).

Like a phoenix, the Web has risen out of cumbersome attempts at large scale experiments that contributed to the development of the Internet and paved the way for hypertext visionaries (Shortlist 6). The Advanced Research Projects Agency (ARPAnet) and MILnet electronically chained together computer networks at several universities and government agencies within a national network to test the validity of electronic communication. Early sharing of electronic files on the Internet and on the Web was made possible by **Internet Protocol (IP)**, and later modes of sharing electronic files by passing through data packets according to the standard of **Transmission Control Protocol (TCP)** came to be known as TCP/IP protocols. Not only did these protocols make transmission and reception methods the same, despite the make or model of computer, but the electronic packaging of information into containers called **packets** sped correspondence, reports, and responses to colleagues within the network.

SHORTLIST 6
Hypertext Visionaries

Jay David Bolter
http://web.uvic.ca/~ckeep/hfl0204.html

Interview with Tim Berners-Lee
http://www.ecn.cz/lee.html

Ted Nelson's Literary Machines
http://web.uvic.ca/~ckeep/hfl0155.html

Ted Nelson and Xanadu
http://www.w3.org./Xanadu.html

Douglas Engelbart's A Conceptual Framework
http:/web.uvic.ca/~ckeep/hf10035.html

George Paul Landow Home Page
http://www.stg.brown.edu/projects/hypertext/landow/cv/landow_ov.html

---

THEORY

Hypertext is a random arrangement of files which may contain words, pictures, icons, and links to other files. The process of hypertext allows users to reorganize and reuse information in any way suited to their needs. Gathered together in smaller webs designated as Web sites, **hyperdocuments** encourage associative thinking in regard to categories and to the sequence of links. Because hypertext documents can always be amended, they are dynamic and evolving. As a medium of expression, hyperdocuments also provide a means to examine other views and to blend other works into our own through links. In a notable initiative, Brown University sponsors George Landow's attempt to develop a web of creative hypertext works as a resource for all. Taking works previously developed in a variety of commercial hypertext programs, Landow and his team of students are translating them into hypertext markup language and then mounting them on the Brown server. Although Douglas Eyman's Digital Space links to his master's thesis, "Introduction: Computers and Composition," and research publications like Texas Tech's *Kairos* journal in order to give a theoretical orientation to hypertext, Landow's site proves the expressive potential of hypertext. Subsequently, Jack Lynch's two sites supply important information and a bibliography about the origin of the book, as well as an index to additional hypertext works and scholarly writings about hypertext (Shortlist 7).

SHORTLIST 7
Hypertext Theory

Douglas Eymand's Digital Space
http://localsonly.wilmington.net/~eymand

Hypertext: An Introduction
http://www.stack.n1/~achie/hypertext/131.html

Hypermedia System
http://osiris.sund.ac.uk/~csOnsa/hyp30004.htm

George Landow's Hypertext Translations
http://www.stg.brown.edu/projects/hypertext/landow/HTatBrown/wwwtrans.html

Jack Lynch's Literary Resources
Bibliography/History of the Book
http://www.english.upenn.edu/~jlynch/Lit/biblio.html

Hypertext
http://www.english.upenn.edu/~jlynch/Lit/hyper.html

Navigating Large Amounts of Text
http://dsmall.www.media.edu/people/dsmall/generals/inspiration.html

Texas Tech's *Kairos* Journal
http://english.ttu.edu/kairos

Hypertext and Writing

Hypertext is changing the way we write. For instance, because it is structureless and fragmentary, as a hypertext **author** you must have the ability to develop a theme but you have the luxury to do so by building a supporting piece at a time. It is like using building blocks to construct the overall design you have in mind. Each block that you add to your design has a purpose and an interrelationship to other contiguous blocks. If you are a hypertext **reader**, you have the ability to reposition the blocks to establish your own relationships; because the blocks are held in virtual space, the structure does not crumble but simply grows.

A second way that hypertext changes the way we write is influenced by new forms of communication introduced by the electronic medium. Each of these forms—e-mail, newsgroups, chat rooms, journal articles, and Web pages—has a set of rules called a **protocol**. Knowing how to follow these protocols increases communication potential.

Another way hypertext alters writing is by increasing the power of expression and challenging the inventive process of both authors and the readers.

For example, a Web page is judged on the basis of its content and context. The content is the written expression conveyed by the unique writing style and tone of the author, but the context establishes a rhetorical effect by means of illustrations, typography, colors and textures, and multimedia elements of animation, sound, and video.

Finally, the traditional stages of the writing process do not always apply to hypertext. For example, an e-mail message is often written spontaneously (on-the-fly), without any revising. Revision occurs when a recipient cuts and pastes comments into the original message. If that message is passed on to others, comments may be added within the original message or tacked on at the end of the text.

Presenting our culture with unparalleled opportunity to preserve itself and to learn about other cultures, hyperdocuments on the World Wide Web preserve vanishing texts, provide public view of rare **artifacts**, and engage other Web users in meaningful discussions of projects and findings. Hypertext, visually augmented by graphics, textures, color, and animation, supplies a compelling new sketchbook for digital rhetoric and presents new issues to resolve. The following chapters introduce you to the World Wide Web, digital rhetoric in hypertext documents, and the rules of this exciting medium of expression.

Through the Looking Glass

The following exercises allow you to explore and draw conclusions about what you see; in essence, you get to be the expert.

WEB LINGO

acceptable use policy (AUP)	hot spots
artifacts	hyperdocuments
author	Hyperties
bookmarks	Intermedia
browser	Internet Protocol (IP)
docuverse	Knowledge Management
database	System (KMS)
graphical user interface (GUI)	Memex

NoteCards   reader
oN Line System(NLS)   Symbolics Document Examiner
packets   Transmission Control Protocol (TCP)
path   UNIX
protocol

TRAVEL ADVISORY

As you travel on the Internet and the World Wide Web take normal tourist precautions:

1. Be careful to whom you give any personal information.
2. Never divulge credit card or social security numbers unless you are sure of the safety of the site.
3. Share your e-mail address, but keep private your password to your account.
4. Read the **acceptable use policy (AUP)** that governs your Internet account and abide by it. Learn what is permitted and how to report infractions of user guidelines to the proper authorities.

TRAVEL TIP: URL

A URL is a zip code that you use to get to different parts of the Web. Each Shortlist calls out URLs. The structure of the URL is simple:

http://www.whitehouse.gov

hypertext   pathway
protocol

Other options in place of **http://** *are:*

file://   for a file on a local drive
ftp://   special site for download files
gopher://   hierarchical site for files
telnet://   remote contact for distant site

TRAVEL TIP: Pointer Functions

The mouse pointer changes depending on its function as a tool:

I   inserts text at this location

↗   selects an object

☞   activates hypertext links

WEB ITINERARY

1. The Memex was a theoretical machine that held information in memory so that its owner could access it at any time. Today we have encyclopedias on CD-ROM. How does the Memex compare to an electronic encyclopedia?

2. Visionaries noted in this chapter created systems that challenged the way we use information and provided a man-machine interface to make finding and using information more efficient. Describe the graphical user interface in this context.

3. As a scientist and a government leader, Vannevar Bush influenced the course of governmental policy toward technology. From the online version of Bush's famous article "As We May Think," determine how Bush felt about knowledge and summarize his reasons for opening up scientific information to a broader audience than scientists.

4. Reviewers of Web sites often write evaluative summaries to advise other users. Travel to Howard Rheingold's site at http://www.well.com/user/hlr/. Write a site report that ranks the site and
   a. Explains the purpose of the site.
   b. Examines how Rheingold orders his information into categories that promote his purpose and appeal to users.
   c. Makes a personal evaluation about the value of the site as a hypertext model.

PROJECT ASSIGNMENT

To begin to understand the collaborative quality of hypertext, have the members of a class turn a piece of notebook paper sideways (landscape) and fold the paper into three equal sections lengthwise. Label each section with

Author, Coauthor, and Categories. Designate an author to respond to a controversial statement. When the author finishes, pass the response to a coauthor who reads and responds to what the author has written. The third person reads the author and coauthor responses and lists major points covered by the two authors. The list of the responses on the categories section becomes a knowledge tree reflecting the content.

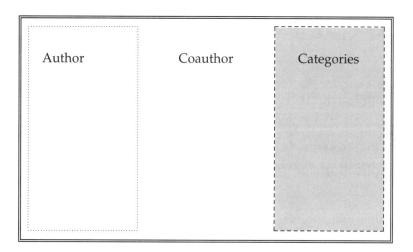

FOR FURTHER READING

"Chapter 1: Conceptual Beginnings of Information Networks." (28 July 1996). <http://www.pacificspirit.com/Courses/WWWCourseDemo/chap1.htm#1>.

Conklin, Jeff. "Hypertext: An Introduction and Survey." *Computer* Sep. 1987: 17–41.

"Hypertext Collaboration: Introduction: Computers and Composition." (28 July 1996). <http://localsonly.wilmington.net/~eymand/fintro.html>.

Leggett, John J., and John L. Schnase. "Viewing Dexter with Open Eyes." Special Issue on Hypermedia. *Communications of the ACM* Feb. 1994: 76–86.

Reddick, Randy, and Elliot King. *The Online Student: Making the Grade on the Internet*. Fort Worth: Harcourt Brace, 1996.

CHAPTER THREE
Web Profile

Origin and Purpose
Growth and Popularity
Internet Components
Implications of the Web

Communication media of the future will accentuate the extensions of our nervous systems, which can be disembodied and made totally collective. New population patterns will fuel the shift from smokestack industries to a marketing-information economy, primarily in the U.S. and Europe. Video-related technologies are the critical instruments of such change.

THE GLOBAL VILLAGE

ORIGIN AND PURPOSE

Throughout history, humans have been captivated by two concepts: time and space. For centuries physicists and philosophers have been at odds with one another as they attempted to describe real time and real space. On the one hand, physicists treat time and space as entities that can be measured and reduced to definable physical laws of the universe so that they may understand how the universe operates. On the other hand, philosophers regard time and space as a container holding the rich tapestry of human experience from which they may examine how the universe ought to operate and develop a theory to guide human thought. In recent years, the emergence of the World Wide Web has challenged old ways of thinking about time and space because the Web does not exist in real time or real space. The World Wide Web exists in cyberspace and its morass of **Web sites** spans a virtual world of computers linked together through modems in a quest for information.

The Web is a virtual community that exists as part of the Internet—a large superstructure of hardware and software interconnection. Growing beyond Tim Berners-Lee's original concept of shareable resources for scientists at CERN, the Web's appeal is due to its ease of use with browsers like Mosaic, Netscape, and Internet Explorer as well as the eye-catching, scrapbook-like presentation of information within hypertext documents.

However, the Web is an anomaly when it comes to statistical analysis. On the one hand, the Web is profitable for businesses that have enterprise sites, but there are no multiyear studies to prove how profitable a corporate Web page is. On the other hand, there appears to be universal agreement that the Web is valuable as a research tool, but there is no comprehensive way of determining who uses it most and for what purpose. From the proliferation of personal Web pages, the Web appears to be a popular medium for self-publishing for true experts and would-be experts, but these Web pages are often sporadic and may disappear as quickly as they appear. In short, we have relied on assumptions or statistical data based on the Internet and related them to the Web, or we have indulged in anecdotes about the Web's potential. Because the Web is a virtual tapestry interweaving sites of commerce with works of art, discourses of conscience, and whimsical listings of personal favorites, its very nature and helter-skelter evolution invite abstraction rather than quantification.

GROWTH AND POPULARITY

To prove the Internet is more than a fad or a fluke, Internet demographers try to determine how it is growing, who is using it, and why it is so popular. Chiefly two kinds of surveys profile Internet sites and users. The first type of survey counts Internet sites and estimates the number of users. In order to start up an **Internet site**, originators of that site register with the Internet Society (InterNIC) by specifying the name and the purpose of the site (commercial, educational, organizational, etc.). Figure 3.1 shows the results of a

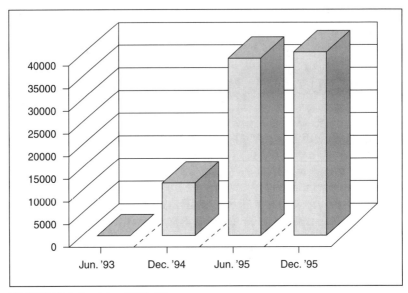

FIGURE 3.1 *Registered Web Sites*

1995 survey that counted registered Web sites. Underscoring the marked increase in Internet sites, the June 1993 figures indicate only 130 sites, but a short 18 months later 11,576 sites are registered, and by June 1995 there are 38,796 sites ("Internet '95" 47).

A description of the site's purpose is required for site registration. If InterNIC accepts the site, it gives the site a domain designation that suits its purpose. For example, *edu* signifies an educational domain. Along with the domain, the site also receives a unique descriptive name to be combined with the domain to create a top-level domain name, like *tcu.edu*. Since it has stopped receiving federal government funds, InterNIC now charges a fee for processing domain names and wants to establish The American Registry for Internet Numbers (http://www.arin.com) to more closely monitor site naming ("Upside to IP Fees" 94). There are two clear advantages to this proposal. First, site names should advertise the purpose of the information found there. Formerly, sites established by individuals purchasing server space from a local Internet provider could call themselves anything because there was no registry process. Individuals could set up sites with domain names common to major corporations and then resell the name to corporations at a profit. A case in point is the use of the site name *whitehouse* which has also been acquired for commercial (.com) and organizational (.org) sites that are far different from the governmental site allowing access to the U.S. president. Second, a more accurate count of sites may be possible. Currently, the Clinton administration is studying how the federal government should serve as a clearinghouse for recordkeeping for the Internet.

Even though the process of naming may not be uniform yet, by understanding top-level domain names, users can anticipate the kind of information that may be available at Web sites. Figure 3.2 lists each domain type and supplies a popular Web site address that contains a simple top-level domain name.

As the Internet branched out to other countries, the three-character domain designation needed to be revised to denote international Web sites. Consequently, international domain names carry a two-character abbreviation of the country's name. Figure 3.3 displays a list of URLs for English versions of virtual art galleries that contain international designators for Canada (*.ca*), the Democratic Republic of Germany (*.de*), France (*.fr*), and the United Kingdom (*.uk*). Although it is rarely used, the United States also has a two character designator, *us*. An appendix provides a complete listing of international domain names.

Counting Internet sites according to domain type reveals trends. After over a decade of compiling statistics, Mark Lottor published an *Internet Domain Survey* that indicated the commercial (*.com*) domain is the largest

DESIGNATOR	PURPOSE	WEB SITE
.com	Commercial	Netscape http://home.netscape.com Microsoft http://www.msn.com
.edu	Educational	Carnegie Mellon College of Humanities and Social Studies http://www.hss.cmu.edu
.gov	Government	White House http://www.whitehouse.gov
.mil	Military	Navy http://www.navy.mil
.net	Network	Galaxy Information Resource http://galaxy.einet.net
.org	Organization	Society for Technical Communication http://www.stc-va.org

FIGURE 3.2 *Top-Level Domain Names for Popular U.S. Sites*

DESIGNATOR	WEB SITE
.ca	Canadian Virtual Museums http://www.civilization.ca/index1e.html
.de	Ruben's Artwork, Web Museum http://www.fhi-berlin.mpg.de/wm/paint/auth/rubens
.fr	The Louvre http://www.culture.fr/cgi-bin/cookie-test-en
.uk	European Cartoon Arts Network http://www.pavilion.co.uk/cartoonet

FIGURE 3.3 *International Domain Names*

with 25.7% followed by the educational (*.edu*) domain at 18.9% ("Surveyors" 70). Even though Lottor has designed several programs to search for and count sites, his statistics are reliable, but approximate. In a count of domestic sites by state for May 1995, New York has the most sites (2,152), closely followed by Massachusetts (2,005), while South Dakota (15) had the fewest. European Hostcount offers raw data based on the number of registered domains on the continent and reflects the amount of change that has occurred since its last monthly sampling. According to the latest available statistics in January 1997, the United Kingdom has experienced the sharpest growth in domain registration followed by Denmark. Monthly statistical growth of registered European domains is increasing steadily. A few sites maintain records of U.S. increases in domain registration. Shortlist 8 provides sites for further investigation of Internet growth statistics.

Internet sites come and go because there is no requirement that once a site is registered it must remain in operation. Consequently, sites can be nonoperational, abandoned, or moved to another Internet address. As hard as it is to keep track of the current number of Internet sites, it is even more difficult to determine the actual number of Internet users by counting them. Therefore, predictions for the number of Internet users range from a conservative five to six million people, to the 1997 Nielsen-CommerceNet survey assertion that "50 million people over the age of sixteen in the U.S. and Canada had Internet access. About 37 million had access to the Web" ("Doing Business" 56).

Seeing a need to subdivide the Internet into three functional parts, Ben Quarterman, a noted Internet expert, characterizes the Core as the main division that includes the Web, the Consumer Internet, and the Matrix which is limited to electronic mail only. According to Quarterman's survey of 1,000

SHORTLIST 8
Internet Statistics

European Hostcount (revised monthly)
http://www.ripe.net/statistics/hostcount.html#dnsdomain

Demographics of Web Users
http://www.digitaldiamond.com/~saunders/demograf.htm

NSFNET Networks by U.S. State (Last updated May 1995)
ftp://nic.merit.edu/statistics/nsfnet/nets.by.state (No longer maintained)

Third MIDS Internet Demographic Survey
http://www3.mids.org/mn/603/ids3sum.html

respondents, the highest concentration of users is age 26–35, closely followed by the 36–45 group with more males represented than females. Another way to divide the Internet is to describe it by its functional areas: the Internet, the Intranet, and the Extranet. While the Internet retains its original function of information sharing and scholarship, the Intranet defines a private Internet established within organizations to promote information sharing, while the Extranet is the newest area for commercial ventures, virtual shopping malls, and speculative business ventures.

Georgia Tech Research Corporation, in conjuction with the Graphic, Visualization, and Usability (GVU) Center of the university, compiled the most credible statistics from surveys over a six-year period to determine who uses the Web and why. In the *Third World Wide Web User Survey*, 13,000 respondents filled in answers to a month-long online survey. From the respondents' answers, the survey showed the median age for American Web users is 36 years old as compared to European Web users who are 31. Men outnumber women by more than a 5 to 1 margin (male users totaled 84.5%; females 15.5%). Respondents earned between $50,000 and $60,000, and over half were married ("Internet '95" 50). Georgia Tech's third survey also probed the frequency and duration of Web exploration as well as the method of exploration according to the demographic characteristics of users. In 1996, GVU conducted a sixth survey calculating answers from 15,000 respondents dealing with the demography of the Web in relation to culture, privacy and censorship issues, and behavior. A special section asked questions about Web administration, service providers, and new programming languages. They found that the average Web user is 35, male, and concerned about data privacy and the speed of Web access. To read the findings yourself, use Shortlist 9.

SHORTLIST 9
Web Survey Resources

Demographics of Users of the World Wide Web
http://www.dnai.com/~bentham/demographics.html

GVU's 3rd WWW User Survey
http://www.cc.gatech.edu/gvu/user_surveys/survey-04-1995/

GVU's 6th WWW User Survey
http://www.cc.gatech.edu/gvu/user_surveys-10-1996/

If the typical Internet user is a working professional with a college degree, who is presumably able to buy the computer and modem to access the Internet ("Caught" 14), the typical Web user is a male, thirty-something professional who most likely appreciates the freedom of travel among Internet components.

INTERNET COMPONENTS

Picturing the Internet as a whole with internal divisions that promote the exchange of information with other users, it is easier to examine the unique features of each of the components (Figure 3.4).

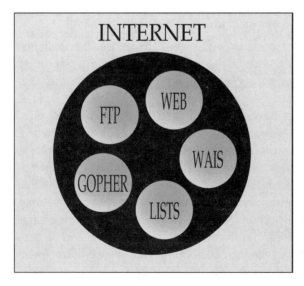

FIGURE 3.4 *Internet Components*

File Transfer Protocol

Our study begins with the oldest component, **file transfer protocol (ftp).** When early Internet innovators established ARAPnet in 1969 as a network of computers to share files regardless of the make of the computers, they used a standard, or protocol, called Internet Protocol (IP). The IP established a common means of transporting information by way of electronic packets from the sending computer to the receiving computer. If a pathway of more than one computer needed to hand off the signal, the routing (router) computer followed the common procedure to transfer the information to its destination, similar to Figure 3.5.

While the IP set up the mode of transferring files, the second Transmission Control Protocol (TCP) monitored and tried to correct any packet-switching errors from the originating computer to the destination computer. For example, if data packets were lost or the packets were received in incorrect order, TCP discovered the problem and corrected it.

Because TCP/IP is the basis of all communication on the Internet, a natural extension of the protocol is a system of uniform procedures for file sharing. With ftp, both text and nontext (binary) files with images, sounds, and videos can be passed on from one computer to another because the computers talk to one another. However, public access to files at an ftp location may be limited. In this way, an Internet site can specify a public directory of files that an anonymous user can explore and from which the user can access public text files, software files, audio files, and multimedia files that are available for downloading. If the files are reserved for only authorized users of the site, or if the site sells memberships, a user may be prompted to supply a password before being able to see an index of files at the location.

Because the files may take up a great deal of memory, they often are shrunk with a software compression program and carry the three-letter extension *.zip.* In order to se the downloaded programs, it may be necessary to have an unzipping program like Pkunzip or Winzip to expand the files on the home computer to which the files have been copied. In this way, the files are reinstated to their original size and become usable on local drives.

Gaining access to an ftp site, finding files, and then copying them formerly required a heady knowledge of the UNIX operating system and its commands.

FIGURE 3.5 *Electronic Transmission of Information*

As the number of ftp sites grew, so did the complexity of locating specific files. As a result, innovators created a search program called Archie that worked in tandem with ftp indexes to scan the sites in order to match keywords entered by a user. Subsequently, Archie gathered a list of likely matching ftp sites that had the files on their indexes. However, Web-based search engines with artful interactive forms prompting for search words or phrases have displaced the code-driven Archie search process because they are more efficient and much easier to use.

Another development with far-reaching implications is the multiple use of the Web browser to reach an ftp site. For example, to access Jean Armour Polly's 1993 Internet guide called "Surfing.2.0.3," the user specifies the type of access (ftp://) followed by the specific ftp address of the Surfing guide in the Netscape location box or the Microsoft Explorer Netsite box, and the browser does all the work (Figure 3.6). Any of the underlined expressions are clickable hypertext links that can be followed by the browser. Moreover, the list associates the size of the file (59 kilobytes with Surfing.2.0.3) and identifies the upload date of the file (the date the author put the file on the ftp site) as well as the type of file (plain text). If the file is a plain or simple text file, a user can load it into any word processing program or read it through the Web browser.

Example:						
Location:	ftp://ftp.nysernet.org/pub/resources/guides/					

At this site, an excerpt from this ftp location looks like this:

Example:

Current directory is /pub/resources/guides

You are located in: /pub/resources/guides

Up to higher level directory

.message	23 bytes	Thu	Apr 14 00:00:00	994	
agguide.dos	86 Kb	Fri	Jul 09 00:00:00	1993	
agguide.wp	105 Kb	Thu	Jun 04 00:00:00	1992	

list continues

surfing.2.0.3	59 Kb	Wed	May 26 00:00:00	1993	Plain Text
whatis.internet	12 Kb	Fri	Jun 19 00:00:00	1992	
zen-1.0.ps	480 Kb	Fri	Jul 09 00:00:00	1993	Postscript Document

FIGURE 3.6 *Reaching an FTP Site*

If the file is copyrighted, it is usually stated on the file. For instance, "Surfing.2.0.3" has this notification on it: "Surfing the INTERNET: an Introduction, Version 2.0.3, Revised May 15, 1993, c. 1992–1993 Jean Armour Polly."

Because the Web browser provides access to ftp lists, downloading capabilities, and uniform standards of operation, institutions are now switching to the Web and no longer maintaining their ftp sites. Of course, there are several reasons for the change. First, ftp sites are difficult for the first-time user to negotiate within a UNIX environment. Second, institutions maintaining two kinds of sites find the duplication expensive and time-consuming. With the intense interest and development concentrated on the Web, the third reason for using Web-based rather than ftp locations is that a Web site allows more frequent and flexible updates of text and graphics to provide more content.

Gopher

The second oldest Internet component is called **gopher**. The funny name comes from the origination point of gopher sites, the University of Minnesota, often called the Mother of all Gophers. The gopher is the mascot of the university and has become the namesake for a site with a highly structured sequence of information, or a topical hierarchy of categories and subcategories. For instance, when university libraries are gophers, they organize their holdings into books, periodicals, and government documents. Each of these categories could yield numerous subcategories that could be searched electronically.

As gopher sites increased, so did the time necessary for manually scanning the site indexes. As a result, a search program called Veronica was designed to scan titles or content of gophers to find matches to user-defined keywords and to provide a list of likely gopher sites. In this area, too, Web-based search engines offer similar search options through a common browser interface. Like ftp, the gopher locations can be accessed through the browser with the type of access (gopher://) followed by the gopher address (yaleinfo.yale.edu) in the Netscape location box or the Microsoft Explorer Netsite box (Figure 3.7). Underlined expressions are clickable links to other files that are described in their title. Gophers can limit access to some files and may offer a program called a Gopher search to find information at the gopher site that matches the user's request. Like ftp sites, gopher sites offer information that can be downloaded; unlike ftp sites, they offer a **gateway** to the third component of the Internet, discussion lists.

Discussion Lists

A **discussion list** is an electronic forum to exchange views. Of the two types of discussion lists, one type is a **newsgroup.** Usenet newsgroups, as they

Example:

Location: gopher://yaleinfo.yale.edu

At this site, an excerpt from this gopher location appears as:

Gopher Menu

***YaleInfo Migration — http://www.yale.edu/yaleinfo ***
About YaleInfo (Visitor View) and Gopher
Announcements
Browse YaleInfo (Yale and Internet Information)

————YALE INFORMATION————
About Yale University (Factsheet)
Alumni Information
Graduate School of Arts & Sciences Admissions Information
Public Affairs News and Resources

FIGURE 3.7 *Searching a Gopher Site*

have come to be called, started in 1979 at Duke University and at the University of North Carolina. A newsgroup consists of Internet users who share similar interests and concerns and who have gone through a sign-up procedure to be part of the newsgroup. As you may imagine, hundreds of online discussion lists exist, ranging from a group that dedicates itself to the study of wine to a group concerned with intellectual property rights. Most of the groups can be divided according to the categories in Figure 3.8. Spinning off the original newsgroups, a number of discussion groups embrace their own

CATEGORY	INTEREST
comp	Computer issues and topics
news	Internet news and issues
rec	Recreation-based topics
sci	Science/technology topics
soc	Political/social topics
talk	Argumentative issues
misc	Broad-ranging topics

FIGURE 3.8 *Newsgroup Main Categories*

CATEGORY	INTEREST
alt	Alternative topics (alien sightings to public trials)
bionet	Biologists' topics
biz	Business news and issues
ieee	Issues related to this professional engineering organization
k12	Instructional issues for primary and secondary schools, teachers, and students

FIGURE 3.9 *Spin-off Groups*

areas of interest and write articles to exchange information. Figure 3.9 offers a selected list of these newer discussion groups.

A newsgroup's member can read, save, print out, or send the article to someone else as an e-mail message. However, the written expression in any article belongs to its author and must be quoted in some form to give credit to the author and to maintain the integrity of the article's expression. Articles are loosely organized into threads that serve to categorize the general topic of discussion. Like a conversation, the discussion can be rambling by taking up tangential topics, or it can be pointed and impassioned.

Although there is Newsreader software available that provides a split screen to select a newsgroup on the first screen and then to see its contents on the second screen, the new features of Netscape Navigator 4 and Internet Explorer 4 make an interface for newsgroups part of the personal Web browsers. In Netscape it is the Collabra application and in Internet Explorer it is Outlook Express. Large corporations and universities on a network generally have Newsreader software available through an arrangement with the Internet administrator.

Although discussions in newsgroups are always public, e-mail messages may be private. In order to successfully interact with other members of the newsgroup, it is important to understand the rules of the particular group and to adhere to common sense precautions of real world communities. Here are some common-sense rules of "netiquette."

Style. Select a descriptive noun phrase to characterize the subject of the article. Avoiding phrases like "general remarks" or "miscellaneous thoughts" is important. If the **post** is a response to another article, the notation *Re:* will precede the subject. Like the subject description, preferred writing style is direct and informal. Whether to use deductive order which puts the major conclusion first or inductive order which draws the major conclusion after careful development of the evidence depends on the author's purpose in writing and the perception of the audience.

Tone.   Tone is another concern. If the attitude conveyed by the writing is arrogant, other members may react unfavorably. By the same token, if the member asks a question or submits a post that is not germane to the current discussion or appropriate to the thread, there may be a harsh response or a **flame** to correct or at least draw attention to the problem. New members should take the time to study a thread and the responses before attempting to originate articles, reply to discussions, ask questions, or second the findings of another.

Arrangement.   Paragraphs still separate groups of coherent thoughts. Because writing is individually expressive, the rule calling for five-paragraph essays may not apply. As brevity is preferred, one-sentence paragraphs are also possible. Punctuation and capitalization help readers of an article understand the association of words and sentences. Logical flow contributes order and reason while it builds credibility for the author. Finally, a signature file (Figure 3.10) enables the author to sign off.

Reading newsgroups involves skimming an index of posts. For example, if the newsgroup is rec.cartoons, typical items are the number of articles displayed versus the total number of articles in the thread, the name or alias of

---

The signature file typically contains the following:

- Author's full name
- Title and organization (if applicable)
- E-mail address

Optional items in a signature can be:

- Voice mail number expressed with area code and phone number separated by periods
- FAX number expressed with periods
- A personally significant proverb or expression

A signature with all of these elements looks like this:
  John Doe
  Human Resource Manager, XYZ Company
  Voice: 901.555.5555
  FAX: 901.555.5556
  E-mail: jdoe@xyx.com
  Innovation starts with a single good idea!

FIGURE 3.10 *Signature File*

Newsgroup: rec.cartoons		Articles: 2 of 21
Larry Beltson	16	television
Mary Alice Wilson	5	adult fantasy

FIGURE 3.11 *Sample Newsgroup Index*

the author, the number of lines in each article, and the descriptive subject supplied by the author (Figure 3.11).

The other type of discussion list is called simply a **list,** and there are two kinds of lists: **moderated** and **automated.** Members who share similar concerns and interests join together to exchange information. If the information is screened by the owner of the list (the moderator), then the list is called a moderated list. Any irrelevant material or inappropriate communication can be excised by the moderator. The automated kind of list is called a **listserv** and its function is to automatically send all incoming information to every member of the list. This is an automated (unmoderated) list because there is no review of the information by the owner of the list.

In order to become a member of a listserv, you must subscribe by sending an e-mail message to the listserv's owner or location. To resign from the listserv, the same type of e-mail notification is used. Expression for the listserv is informal and spontaneous, with the online community responding to issues or to questions put to the group. Standard English and punctuation apply as well as prudent expression of ideas and reactions in conversational messages to members of the listserv. Postings to these lists are e-mail transmissions and can have larger electronic documents attached to them. Current technology in browser software also permits active hypertext links to be included. Here is an excerpt from a message posted to e-com, a listserv devoted to writing teachers. The discussion question from Nancy Stegall at DeVry Institute in Phoenix invites participation from the group:

> How are you all doing with faculty training? If you find yourself as busy as we are in Phoenix, creating training opportunities is a real struggle. Has anyone come across any good ideas?

Wide Area Information Service

A fourth type of Internet component is the **Wide Area Information Service (WAIS).** It works like a periscope because it scans all the indexes of accumulated information in databases and identifies relevant articles on the basis of whether their content matches a phrase in a query statement typed in by the user. WAIS can operate up above the sea of data or within it to search in a hierarchical sequence until it finds all the articles matching a user's query. However, improvements in Web search technology mean that Web-based search engines can simulate WAIS performance.

World Wide Web

The fifth Internet component is, of course, the World Wide Web. As the newest component of the Internet, the Web began in 1991 as a gesture of good will and corporate efficiency when Tim Berners-Lee created it for his colleagues to exchange information about their projects at CERN, a research laboratory in Europe. Part of the charm of the Web is that it seems organic, without structure, and open to public development. Whereas ftp, gopher, WAIS, and discussion groups are controlled by some institution or owned by an individual, the Web is owned by the community that uses it.

With the creation of affordable graphical browsers like Mosaic, Netscape, and Internet Explorer to conceal complex programming statements, the Web has become the place to travel. Most importantly, because of the browsers' universal access to gopher sites, ftp sites, or discussion lists, the World Wide Web is the starting location for new users and a viable destination for businesses, educational institutions, and private citizens who want to be part of the dynamic growth and potential market.

IMPLICATIONS OF THE WEB

The Web holds enormous appeal for Internet users because it possesses a range of possibilities. Personally, it offers a place to publish one's thoughts and drawings, to read and comment on the work of others, or to simply indulge in the whimsy of the moment. Professionally, the Web provides a way to do research and to associate with others who may offer worthwhile advice. Commercially, the Web offers a new venue for goods and services from banking to entertainment. Culturally, the Web is a milieu of beliefs and values as well as an archive of artifacts which help us understand one another. Technologically, the Web is a test bench for new graphical browsers like Netscape and Internet Explorer or new applications offered for free public trial by gifted entrepreneurs. Politically, the Web is a troublesome entity that calls into question time-honored concepts of free speech, fair use, and capitalism. Historically, the Web is a community defining itself in a global context. As a community of people who communicate with one another through Web pages, e-mail, or lists, the Web is truly publicly owned and operated.

The Web consists of layers of hypertext documents which can hold text, images, sound files, video files, and links to other documents. Hypertext documents are joined together by software links that span virtual space in a click of a mouse button. To get to any specific location, a user must understand the structure of a digital zip code, the URL. For instance, a URL bears a top-level domain name, and sometimes a server identification (the institution which has a Web site), a directory pathway (names of directories/subdirectories that the message must pass through), and a specific file or account location. URLs have various arrangements of these elements that are joined together in a sequence of characters and punctuation. Correctly typing in the URL in lowercase letters with strict attention to the sequence and punctuation is necessary because the graphical browsers will look for the location based only on what the user enters. In this regard, their search is context sensitive. Occasionally, URLs will include capitals, a tilde (~), a colon (:), an underscore (_), a percent (%), and/or a hyphen (-). Figure 3.12 shows a simple URL for the U.S. House of Representatives.

To get to the Web site of the U.S. House of Representatives, this URL would have to be entered into a graphical browser in the exact sequence. Although some URLs are simple, others are long and tedious to type. The Consumer Information Catalog listing government publications for purchase or for downloading has a long URL: http://www.gsa.gov/staff/pa/cic/. When the URL is entered into a graphical browser, the connection goes to the government top-level domain location, then through the General Services Administration (*gsa*) directory, and then through subdirectories (*staff*, *pa*, *cic*) to arrive at the catalog page (Figure 3.13).

As the most recent of the five Internet components, the Web has experienced rapid growth that can be measured by the number of new Web servers registered to the six domains: commercial, educational, governmental, military, network resources, and organizational. As a network of hypertext documents, the Web has potential for dynamic informational retrieval and the flexibility of accessing other Internet components.

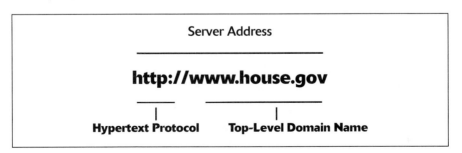

FIGURE 3.12 *U.S. House of Representatives Home Page*

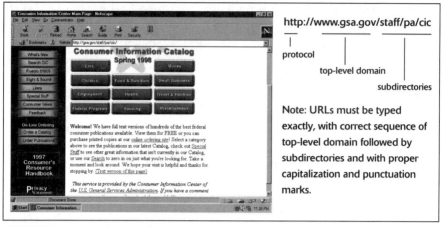

FIGURE 3.13 *Lengthy URL for Consumer Information Catalog*

Because the Web can be an important means for students to acquire information, ask advice, seek out new theories, and gain free documents and software, the rest of this textbook explains the potential benefits and technological tools of the Web as well as the technique of a discovery journal. More accurate than keeping track of site addresses with jotted notations, the discovery journal is an effective recordkeeping tool that helps users remember what they found and why it will be important to visit again. The journal is a list of URLs, site names, and personal evaluations that can be invaluable in retracing the path to useful information on the Web.

Through the Looking Glass

The following exercises allow you to explore and draw conclusions about what you see; in essence, you get to be the expert.

WEB LINGO

context sensitive   download
discussion list   flame

gateway	listserv
file transfer protocol (ftp)	Web Sites
gopher	Wide Area Information Service (WAIS)
lists (moderated, automated)	Internet site
newsgroup	post

TRAVEL TIP: Discovery Journal

Create a discovery journal to help you remember sites and to record important information that can be used to document each site.

1. From the Windows ™ desktop, open the Accessories group.
2. From the Accessories group, select the program NotePad or WordPad.
3. Open the program and type your name on the first line. Hit enter and type the nature of your discovery, like "Search for hypertext sources." On the next line, type in the date of your Web exploration.
4. Determine a beginning URL and type it into the file.
5. In the top right-hand corner of the program's screen you will see three small icons:
   - a minus sign (stores program on the taskbar for quick retrieval)
   - a box or two boxes (maximize/minimize the size of the current program's screen)
   - an X (closes program)

   Use the minus sign to store the NotePad or WordPad program on the Windows taskbar.
6. Open the browser, search for your first URL.
7. Double click on the NotePad or WordPad program stored on the taskbar and type in the exact name of the site, its author, and date of creation or update. Add your evaluation of the site.
8. When you've made your notations, click on the minus sign to store the NotePad or WordPad program on the taskbar.
9. At the end of your search, save your discovery journal as a text (.txt) file with an eight character name that describes the nature of the search; for example: hypertxt.txt.

SHORTCUT KEYS: **ALT Tab** (Calls up previous window)
CTRL C (Copies highlighted text or object)
CTRL V (Pastes copied text or object)

Here is an excerpt from a discovery journal about hypertext theory. Notice that each site starts with the URL followed by the site name, author (if known), date of creation or update, and e-mail contact information. Important links forward or backward are noted along with a personal evaluation.

Gerry Adams
Hypertext Theory Research
July 1997_____
http://www.cl.cam.ac.uk/users/gdr11/style-guide.html
Style guide
Gareth Rees, April 1996.
discusses a view of hypertext design to include easy use and better content rather than rigid structure
e-mail: Gareth.Rees@cl.cam.ac.uk

http://www.ualberta.ca/~ckeep/hfl0267.html
Electronic Labyrinth
Christopher Keep, et al.
hypertext works with active links in a chronology

http://www.w3.org/pub/WWW/People/Berners-Lee/
Tim Berners-Lee Home Page with his bio and photo
e-mail: timbl@w3.org
Link to: http://www.w3.org/pub/DataSources/bySubject/Overview.html
    WWW Virtual Library

WEB ITINERARY

1. Using your browser, travel to the popular Web sites listed in Figure 3.2. Write a brief description that includes the name, the purpose of the site, and your evaluation of each site.
2. Figure 3.3 is a list of international sites for virtual galleries. Travel to these sites and compose a travel brochure for your classmates that names and describes the content of each site.
3. Visit the historical site at ftp.nysernet.org/pub/resources/guides. Download the file *surfing.2.0.3*. How have the advantages offered by the Internet changed since the essay was written in 1993?

4. Develop a questionnaire to test Internet literacy. You may ask people to identify vocabulary words in the first two chapters, guess at the number of users, or comment about the worth of the Information Superhighway. Distribute the questionnaire to a target group in your educational institution. After you total and interpret responses, report your findings to the class.

5. Refer to Georgia Tech's GVU's 6th WWW User Survey at http://www. cc.gatech.edu/gvu/user_surveys-10-1996/. According to the findings, predict who will be the users of the Web in the year 2000.

PROJECT ASSIGNMENT

Since the Web is dynamic, its profile changes quickly. Several individuals have devoted their time to compiling statistics about the Internet and about the Web. Check out these sites. (Upper- and lower-case elements form these URLs.) Make a note if you encounter any nonfunctioning sites. You may save the textual information as plain text files on your own disk drive by using the browser option File, Save As.

Assimilating statistics from these URLs, write an analytical paper that profiles the current status of World Wide Web and its users.

http://www.internic.net
http://nw.com/zone/WWW/top.html (latest survey results July 1996)
http://www.genmagic.com/Internet/Trends/slide-4.html
http://www.nw.com/zone/WWW/report.html
http://www.mids.org (latest survey)
http://www.mit.edu:8001/people/mkgray/net/
http://www.ripe.net/statistics/hostcoutn.html#dnsdomain
http://www.cc.gatech.edu/gvu/user_surveys/survey-10-1996
http://www.webcom.com/~walsh

FOR FURTHER READING

The Arts: Landscape of Our Time. Phi Theta Kappa Honors Study Topic Program Guide, 1996–97.
Bournellis, Cynthia. "Internet '95." *Internet World* Nov. 1995: 47+.

Clark, Michael. *Cultural Treasures of the Internet.* Upper Saddle River, NJ: Prentice-Hall, 1995.

Kambil, Ajit. "Doing Business in the Wired World." *Computer* May 1997: 56–61.

Snyder, Joel. "Upside to IP Fees." *Internet World* Apr. 1997: 84–85.

CHAPTER FOUR

Archives & Artifacts

Types of Informational Structures

General Reference Sites

Published Texts

> *Anyone who has been involved in gestalt, or studied primitive societies—once he or she gets over the impulse to measure these societies with Western templates—is aware that either-or is not the only possibility. Both-and can also exist.*
>
> THE GLOBAL VILLAGE

TYPES OF INFORMATIONAL STRUCTURES

In addition to being classified by domain, sites can be classified according to the structure of information they provide. There are five types of informational structures, which we will identify throughout this chapter in conjunction with our discussion of general reference sites. Whether the site is a virtual museum, a digital library, or a municipal archive, a Web author will decide on an arrangement that clearly and directly presents the content in keeping with the purpose of the site. Therefore, in the following list you will see informational structures identified by functional arrangement:

- **Umbrella** (all-in-one) sites attempt to provide hypertext links to all other similar Web locations.
- **Topic-specific** sites have a single unifying theme with links to similar sites.
- **Searchable** sites have so much information that an internal program attached to the site scans it to find matching data to user-defined keywords.
- **FAQ,** or frequently asked questions sites, anticipate and give answers to relevant questions about the site, its purpose, and its operation.
- **Expressive** sites share personal experiences, preferences, and forecasts.

Gaining knowledge is an idiosyncratic process; we all have our own way of learning. The Web enables all users to learn according to their own style and at their own pace, whether it means learning something new, seeing something in a different light, or even asking advice or sharing experiences.

GENERAL REFERENCE SITES

The Web is a resource for self-help and self-publishing. Not only have academic institutions and government agencies committed time and energy to recasting dictionaries, library holdings, electronic books and magazine collections, course syllabi, and college writing centers into digital **archives,** but publishers, corporations, and online communities have also contributed catalogs, magazines, technical reports/papers, counseling areas, and public forums.

Dictionaries

As a starting point for the investigation of a term or a concept, the dictionary has long been an authoritative source of word derivation and meaning. Traditionally, a word, its pronunciation, history, and various meanings are all part of an entry in a dictionary. However, when a dictionary is transferred to the Web, there are a few adaptions to suit the online presentation. The first adaption is a flexible entry point. With printed dictionaries, finding a definition means thumbing through pages of alphabetic entries. In a Web document, finding a term may mean clicking on a hypertext link, which is denoted by colored text and an underline, or may mean using a search tool to locate the term in a large hypertext document and then to display it with its definition. Here is a contrasting model to explain the difference between a **linear** presentation of a print-based dictionary and the **nonsequential** access of a hypertext dictionary.

Print-based Definition

¹**Mouse**\'maůs*n, pl.* mice\'mīs\ [ME, fr. OE *mūs;* akin to OHG *mūs,* mouse, L *mus,* GK *mys* mouse, muscle] (bef. 12c) **1:** any of numerous small rodents (as of the genus Mus) with pointed snout, rather small ears, elongated body, and slender tail **2:** a timid person **3:** a dark-colored swelling caused by a blow; specif: BLACK EYE **4:** a small mobile manual device that controls movement of the cursor and selection of functions on a computer display

Hypertext Definition

Mouse
Definition
Pronunciation
Jargon
Word Derivation
Other Usage
    └ hypertext links to
        other text files

Two characteristics of the hypertext display are readily apparent. First, the amount of text is minimalized. Second, the reading order is random and totally controlled by the user who determines which link to click on. Because hypertext dictionaries are an efficient means to learn new terms and an excellent initial step for research, reports, and course papers, here are a few of the most interesting sites in Shortlist 10.

An example of a comprehensive hypertext dictionary is an umbrella site. As its name implies, the List of Dictionaries provides hypertext links to most

---

SHORTLIST 10
Dictionary Archives

List of Dictionaries
http://math-www.uni-paderborn.de/dictionaries/Dictionaries.html

Logical World of Etymology
http://www.bit.net/~melanie//thelogic.htm

A Web of On-line Dictionaries
http://www.bucknell.edu/~rbeard/diction.html

Yahoo Knowledge Tree
http://www.yahoo.com/Reference/Dictionaries

QUICK LOOK-UP (ENGLISH)
Enter word here: [   ]

FIGURE 4.1 *Look-Up Box for Online Dictionary*

online dictionaries. Not only is this a popular Web location as indicated by the high number of visitors on the **counter,** it is also a high-quality site as indicated by the numerous award icons.

Recognized for its thoroughness, attractive informational design, and ease of use, this site from Germany (international domain name *.de*) provides links to a myriad of online dictionaries ranging from standard dictionaries to translation sources to computer jargon dictionaries. Although the List of Dictionaries site is convenient to look up words, a topic-specific site that is devoted to short essay descriptions of terms is The Logical World of Etymology. The approach of the **site owner** is to give written responses to visitors' questions about word derivation. Another plus is its bibliography of printed resources related to etymology. As a searchable site, Bucknell University's Web of On-line Dictionaries offers a quick look-up box (Figure 4.1). A user types in the term and presses the enter key to activate the search. There are also links to online reference resources which may prove valuable when finding definitions for terms and expressions.

Libraries

The **digital library** is an outgrowth of Vannevar Bush's original theory about sharing knowledge when he was the presidential Science Advisor in 1945. His proposal for the Memex envisioned a retrieval process that would allow users of the machine to randomly access documents and annotate them. Although Bush is known as the Father of Hypertext, Ted Nelson coined the term *hypertext* and extended the theory to practical applications at Brown University in the 1960s. His vision and computer systems became the core of initiatives for digital libraries.

A digital library is a collection of documents and artifacts retained in **cyberspace.** By 1993, there was significant growth of digital libraries, especially on college campuses, and in the establishment of new criteria for library organization based on hypermedia. With emerging technology, libraries could offer an index of holdings via hypertext links or spatial orientations to book collections through locator maps. In this sense, a global system of libraries could begin with the integration of digital library projects throughout the world.

Library of Congress.   Important in the digital library initiative is the venerable Library of Congress, which revolutionized the retrieval processes of collection libraries with its card catalog system at the beginning of the twentieth century. Today it is setting the pace for other libraries as it strives to reach its goal of digitizing half a million documents by the end of this century (Amdur 33). The Library of Congress Web site (Figure 4.2) is both an umbrella site and a searchable site. Originally structured in a hierarchical list as a gopher index, the site is now organized into a colorful blend of images and text that are links to a myriad of hypertext documents. Of particular interest are the well-developed virtual exhibits hosted by the Library of Congress.

Not only does this site illustrate the high quality possible in a large hypertext document, but its visually arranged categories use images that describe the content and demonstrate a superb combination of text, graphics, and technical functionality. For instance, **informational flow** starts with a photograph of the building and landscape, followed by a series of **hot buttons** with options printed on them. By positioning the mouse pointer over the category and clicking, the screen changes to subject matter of the category.

Another important government repository is the U. S. Census Bureau with population information that changes with each new birth to update both world and U.S. population figures automatically. Characterized as a userfriendly archive of statistics, this site invites exploration because it is simple

FIGURE 4.2 *Library of Congress*

SHORTLIST 11
Government Archives

Library of Congress
http://lcWeb.loc.gov/homepage

Library of Congress Exhibits
http://lcWeb.loc.gov/homepage/exhibits.html

U.S. Census Bureau
http://www.census.gov

---

and easy to use and because its information is reliable and regularly updated. It too is organized as a series of hot buttons, with clearly defined topic areas.

Both government repositories (Shortlist 11) are popular topic-specific sites because they possess important attributes for a credible site:

1. They show a logical arrangement of information in a pleasing design that invites users to explore.
2. The information they provide is current and accurate.
3. Their content is well developed.
4. Links to other sites or links within the site's files are current and accurate. In essence, these sites attract a high volume of users because the authors take pains to keep them accurate, current, germane, and continually functional. The Library of Congress Exhibits are superior online, and often interactive, sites with well-researched content that the general reading public finds interesting and informative. The Census Bureau is equally captivating with its storehouse of statistics and its changing population counter.

University Libraries.   Experimentation in digital library technology has also been boosted by state-of-the-art experiments in information technology at universities. Funded in part by the National Science Foundation and by a partnership with corporations, many universities have developed software capable of emulating quite a few library functions. Among the institutions establishing digital libraries, Carnegie Mellon University and the University of California at Berkeley have published attractive and functional Web home pages which allow public scanning of holdings while reserving password-only use of certain areas for faculty, staff, and students of the institutions. Among universities pursuing digital library initiatives, library holdings vary

---

SHORTLIST 12
University Libraries

Carnegie Mellon
http://www.library.cmu.edu

Columbia (Project Bartleby)
http://www.columbia.edu/acis/bartleby

University of California, Berkeley
http://www.lib.berkeley.edu

University of Illinois
http://www.grainger.uiuc.edu

---

from fully digitized books to collections and special rare book holdings. Carnegie Mellon University allows public browsing of its specialized libraries like the Hunt Library for business and the humanities or the Engineering and Science Library which links to scientific journals and books. UC Berkeley offers a spatial orientation to the physical locations on campus with a table of clickable library names serving as **active links** to a street map of their locations. Shortlist 12 contains a selected list of digital libraries that are all topic-specific sites.

Collaborative Libraries. Municipalities, educational institutions, government agencies, and corporations have joined together in a **consortium** to design and implement digital libraries for special holdings. Since their efforts create opportunities to see and learn about the human race and culture, browsing their contents is very worthwhile. Shortlist 13 lists digital collections that are all topic-specific sites.

Several examples reveal the amazing diversity of the Web ventures. EXPO offers a virtual bus ride to the Dead Sea pavilion of the Library of Congress. This is an ambitious venture to gather together fragile and rare, early books for unprecedented public viewing on a Web page. This library has a picture of each manuscript with a summary of its historical significance. Another example is the National Aeronautical and Space Administration's Web (NASA Library) and its arrangement of hot buttons for virtual areas that provide launch footage, lunar pictures, and technical reports. Finally, the New York Public Library (Figure 4.3) provides library services and answers to typical questions with a handsomely redesigned page that serves local and remote patrons.

SHORTLIST 13
Collaborative Libraries

Alexandria Digital Library
http://alexandria.sdc.ucsb.edu/

EXPO Ticket Office
http://sunsite.unc.edu/expo/ticket_office.html

Great Composers
http://classicalmus.com/

Internet Public Library
http://ipl.sils.umich.edu

NASA Library
http://www.nasa.gov/hqpao/library.html

New York Public Library
http://www.nypl.org

Smithsonian Institute
http://www.si.edu

W3C World Wide Web Consortium
http://www.w3.org

FIGURE 4.3 *The New York Public Library. Reprinted, by permission, from the New York Public Library.*

PUBLISHED TEXTS

Six forms of digitally published texts exist:

- Electronic books
- Electronic journals/newspapers
- Personal magazines, or **zines**
- Advice and feedback
- Personal Web pages
- Correspondence

Although the quality of the content and writing style varies, each form offers a unique forum to express ideas, values, and beliefs. As a result, a digitally published text can be anything from a sleek, multicolor business magazine, to a scholarly anthology with hypertext links to other scholarly essays, to a writing center's assessment of a student's essay, to a position paper from an individual or activist group, to a discussion between Web users, and finally to an individually crafted Web page compiling inspiring passages or listing personal achievements.

Electronic Books

Mass production of bound books dates back to the 1500s when the printing press made bound texts widely available. The advent of printing technology marked a departure from the time-honored traditions in which some cultures laboriously hand copied manuscripts while other cultures used spoken prose and poetry to keep alive the history of their people and descriptions of their civilizations.

A similar revolution is now underway. In an effort to share literature, to preserve the classics, and to experiment with interactive hyperdocuments, universities have led the way in digitally transcribing printed texts into electronic texts. In 1971, Michael Hart created *Project Gutenberg,* with a thirty-year goal of transposing 10,000 books into digital form for the public. Not only did those involved in this initiative have to digitize thousands of words from existing books, they also had to figure out how to retain the integrity of the literary work while making full use of the electronic media. Other book projects took shape like *Alex Catalogue of Electronic Books* and *Wiretap.* Although *Project Gutenberg* and *Wiretap* are the best-known repositories of electronic books, Shortlist 14 includes sites that have classical and nonclassical works online. These books can be viewed on the screen or downloaded to disk or printer and they may be found at an ftp site or a gopher site, in addition to a Web site.

SHORTLIST 14
Electronic Book Archives

Alex Catalogue of Electronic Texts
http://www.lib.ncsu.edu/staff/morgan/alex/alex-index.html

CMU English Server
http://english-www.hss.cmu.edu/

Electronic Text Center
http://www.lib.virginia.edu/texts.html (access may be restricted)

Wiretap Online Library
http://ftp.sunet.se/ftp/pub/etext/wiretap-classic-library

Project Gutenberg
http://www.promo.net/pg/

With the unlimited potential for free public dissemination of books over the Web, print-based texts converted to online books have called into question current interpretations of copyright laws. Some sites, including those in Shortlist 14, may require a password or subscription before allowing access to online books. Other sites may allow access, but require signing a guestbook to leave an e-mail address.

Electronic Journals/Newspapers

An electronic journal is a hypertext version of a print-based document like *Business Week,* which appeals to the public, or *Internet World,* which appeals to an emerging class of virtual citizens. Both of these publications are found via an umbrella site called The Electronic Newstand. To make things easier, Web browsers, including the newest versions of Netscape and Internet Explorer, group together colorful icons that are clickable hypertext links to publications like the *Interactive Wall Street Journal.*

Not all Web publications contain the full content of the print-based version. Indeed, some publications will consist of abstracts and supply information about subscribing to the online publication for a full-text version. In addition, a few popular electronic periodicals like *Hot Wired* require that you register with a full name and working e-mail account before you can access the site's information. Shortlist 15 contains online versions of popular magazines.

An electronic journal can also be a scholarly publication that is transferred from a print medium or specially crafted for a hypertext medium. Scholarly

SHORTLIST 15
Electronic Periodicals

Byte
http://www.byte.com

Business Week
http://www.businessweek.com/indexl.html

Electronic Newsstand
http://www.enews.com

Internet World Online
http://www.internetworld.com/

Mother Jones
http://mojones.com/mother_jones/mother_jones.html

National Geographic Online
http://nationalgeographic.com/contents/

Scientific American
http://www.sciam.com/

Wall Street Journal
http://info.wsj.com/
(subscription required)

Wired
http://www.hotwired.com/

journals can be issued by a professional society, by a group of interested researchers, or by a consortium of academic institutions. The venerable *Chronicle of Higher Education* is a good illustration of a print-based resource for academia going digital. Originally a gopher site, the *Chronicle*'s reference publication *Academe This Week* consists of textual links to article summaries of the *Chronicle*, selected indexes on books, technology updates, and job listings in the current issue. Other available scholarly publications range in disciplines from science and mathematics to composition and communication. Shortlist 16 has a sampling of scholarly journal resources.

Because scholarly publications are written with an expert user in mind, the vocabulary and the complexity of the concepts they contain may be daunting. However, the author may invite inquiries or comments or may provide a useful bibliography with links to other online documents. An ambitious project is the *Scholarly Communication Project* at Virginia Tech, which contains

---

SHORTLIST 16
Scholarly Journals

WWW Virtual Library
http://www.edoc.com/ejournal/

English Language and Literature
http://www.lib.vt.edu/lib/armstrong/English_L&L.html

Classics Alcove
http://nervm.nerde.ufl.edu/~blaland/Class.html

List of Lists
http://catalog.com/vivian/interest-group-search.html

Omnimedia Links
http://www.awa.com/library/omnimedia/links.html

---

interesting reading concerning electronic journals. The response of the academic community to this form of publishing is in an online proposal *Scholarly Electronic Journals—Trends and Academic Attitudes: A Research Proposal* by McEldowney, Shontz, and Wright. Acknowledging the rising cost of print-based documents, the declining costs of technology to produce and maintain electronic documents, and the allure of group- or self-publishing opportunities, these scholars seem to view the last five years as a clear indication of the importance and popularity of scholarly publications on the Internet and the Web. They also believe that scholarly publishing will gain additional authors as more professors discover how their works can be transferred to the electronic medium. Certainly, the number of scholarly sites has increased as Shortlists 17 and 18 demonstrate.

Zines

The Web is an exciting place for self-published work. The zine is an expressive document expounding the values and beliefs of the individual author or themes endorsed by an interest group that sponsors the Web site. Although these sites may be more anecdotal than factual, they can provide a unique outlook or a fresh approach to issues and events. An umbrella site called E-zines has been carefully developed over several years at the O'Reilly Publications site and provides timely updates. Of course, zines may disappear as quickly as they appear, but the URLs in Shortlist 18 reflect recent listings.

SHORTLIST 17
Scholarly Publications

Academe This Week
http://chronicle.merit.edu

Animation Journal
http://www.chapman.edu/animation/

Film and History
http://www.h-net.msu.edu/~filmhis/

Resources for Feminist Research
http://www.oise.on.ca/rfr/

Scholarly Communications Project
http://scholar.lib.vt.edu/

Scholarly Electronic Journals—Trends and Academic Attitudes: A Research Proposal
http://poe.acc.virginia.edu/~pm9k/libsci/ejs.html

THES: Post Gutenberg Galaxy
http://cogsci.ecs.soton.ac.uk/%7Eharnad/THES/thes.html

Transactions of the Kansas Academy of Science
http://www.emporia.edu/S/www/kas/transact.htm

SHORTLIST 18
Zines

E-zines
http://www.dominis.com/zines

Web Zines
http://webreference.com/magazines.html

Zines Zines Everywhere
http://thetransom.com/chip/zines/

SHORTLIST 19
Help and Service Sites

AskERIC
http://ericir.syr.edu/

Brandeis Hiatt Career Center
http://www.brandeis.edu/hiatt/

FedWorld (federal job posting)
http://www.fedworld.gov

National Writing Centers Association
http://departments.colgate.edu/diw/NWCA.html

Monster Board (hi-tech job posting)
http://www.monster.com/

Purdue Online Writing Lab
http://owl.english.purdue.edu

Weather Browser (Interactive)
http://rs560.cl.msu.edu/weather/

Advice and Feedback

The Web has unique centers to help others by providing advice and informa-tion. The examples in Shortlist 19 illustrate the divergent approaches such centers take. As a **clearinghouse** for publications, AskERIC's searchable data-base can help build a working bibliography of sources which may be found in a college library or elsewhere on the Web. The Interactive Weather Browser at Michigan State University supplies maps showing the weather for a user-specified area of the United States as well as climate statistics and forecasts. Even though Brandeis University reserves a portion of its Hiatt Career Center site for students and alumni, it is a valuable resource for the way it categorizes career fields and attempts to give comprehensive hyper-text links to job lists for each career field. As an umbrella site, the Hiatt Career Center links to the Monster Board and FedWorld. Finally, if the Purdue Online Writing Lab offered only its list of English resources in language and grammar, that would be enough. However, the National Writing Centers Association links to all online writing services, of which the oldest writing center is the Purdue OWL. The Purdue OWL is a springboard for a **newbie** learning how to research on the Internet because the OWL supplies a very

---

SHORTLIST 20
FAQs

Search FAQs
http://www.lib.ox.ac.uk/search/search_faqs.html

Robotics FAQ
http://www.cs.indiana.edu/robotics/FAQ/copy.html

---

useful set of hypertext links to online manuals that define and describe the Internet and the Web.

Yet another form of advice site is provided in an **FAQ,** which is either an arrangement of pithy questions followed by specific answers or a summary of terms, symptoms, or misconceptions, which then link to explanations at other Web sites. Actually, FAQs have been around for some time. When the Internet was in its infancy, FAQs were a handy means to provide **plain text** instructions or answers to likely questions for new users of a site. One of the FAQs in Shortlist 20 is topic-specific and gives advice about robotics, while the other FAQ provides a search engine to find more FAQs.

Personal Web Pages

A Web page is an artifact that exists in virtual space to publicly give information in text and pictures. Corporations, educational institutions, and government agencies have developed very elaborate home pages in vivid colors of text played against rich backgrounds of images. Whereas these home pages act as ornate portals to vast databases, the personal home pages that have proliferated over the past three years afford individuals a creative outlet to air their personal beliefs, values, and reactions. A personal Web page is a self-published electronic document meant to manifest knowledge, insight, preferences, or even mark meaningful events within the Web community. By its very nature as a malleable product of individual taste, the personal Web page is always experimental and dynamic.

Web building is an important extension of self-expression and a measure of Web mastery. The next two chapters teach you how to find information at Web sites related to your interest area. Two later chapters introduce hypertext markup language as a means to code Web pages.

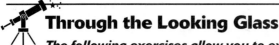

Through the Looking Glass

The following exercises allow you to explore and draw conclusions about what you see; in essence, you get to be the expert.

WEB LINGO

archives	hot buttons
active links	informational flow
clearinghouse	linear
consortium	newbie
counter	nonsequential
digital library	plain text
FAQ (frequently asked question)	site owner
home pages	zines

TRAVEL TIP: Focusing a Search

Create a discovery journal that will record sites and artifacts.

1. In the browser location/netsite box, type in the URL for a simple-to-use search engine like Yahoo (URL: http://www.yahoo.com).
2. When the Yahoo screen appears, type in the keywords to describe your interest area in the Search box, or use the categories of information in the knowledge tree to find Web sites related to your interest area.

Text and artwork copyright © 1998 by Yahoo! Inc. All rights reserved. YAHOO! and the YAHOO! logo are trademarks of YAHOO! Inc.

3. Create a discovery journal related to your interest area by copying URLs, site descriptions, and contact information to a NotePad or WordPad file.

4. As you come across a picture of a person or an artifact that you think will be important to your work, use the capture feature of the browser to save the artifact to a floppy disk. Remember to also record the URL and site information where the picture was found. Images may be copyrighted and cannot be used publicly without permission of the owner.

Capturing a Picture.   In Netscape, position the mouse pointer over the picture displayed in the browser and click on the right mouse button to bring up the Save Image As menu. In the dialog box that appears showing the original name of the image, make sure that the correct drive is indicated as the destination.

In Internet Explorer, position the mouse pointer over the picture displayed in the browser and click on the right mouse button to bring up the Save Target As menu. In the dialog box that appears showing the original name of the image, make sure that the correct drive is indicated as the destination.

In either browser, click the Save button.

WEB ITINERARY

1. Explore the Library of Congress Special Exhibit 1492. Write a short paper that summarizes the content of this exhibit.

2. Visit the National Writing Centers Association home page and the Purdue Online Writing Center. Write a report to your classmates to explain the purpose of these sites and three important services to help students' writing.

3. Explore the university libraries suggested in Shortlist 12. Write an evaluation in which you rank the libraries on organization, information content, accuracy, and credibility of information.

4. Use the career-related sites listed in Shortlist 19 to find information on a career field that you want to pursue. Determine how the virtual job market will change career planning and report back to the class.

PROJECT ASSIGNMENT

Develop a discovery journal using the Yahoo search engine to find Web sites that may suit all of the informational structures (umbrella sites, topic-specific, searchable, FAQ, and expressive) related to your major area of study.

Record the information on a NotePad or WordPad file. Here is a sample discovery journal based on the humanities discipline.

Anne Kelley
Humanities Resources Search—Yahoo Search Engine
1-12-97

WWW Virtual Library Humanities Page
http://www.hum.gu.se/w3vl/w3vl.html
Contents include links to Indexes, Archaeology, History, Philosophy, Religion, Languages and Literature and others that include exhibitions/libraries/museums/publications
****

Scholarly Internet Resource Collections, University of California http://lib-www.ucr.edu/rivera/
A search engine that uses keyword, subject, title searches to find specific humanities artifacts
****

Humanities Hub, Griffith University, Brisbane, Australia
http://www.gu.edu.au/cgi-bin/g-code?/gwis/hub/qa/hub.home.html
A search engine with a knowledge tree for a large number of social science and humanities resources
****

UNCA Humanities Resources
http://www.unca.edu/humanities/hum.links.html
Links to individual artists like Virgil, Chaucer, Shakespeare, Mark Twain (Jim Zwick page at Syracuse University that includes music and an excellent compilation of resources http://Web.syr.edu/~fjzwick/twainwww.html)
****

Humanities Resources on the Internet
http://www.sil.org/humanities/resources.html
Includes links to HUMBUL Gateway, books, English/linguistic/rhetoric/writing resources as well as university departments, professional societies, publications, computing resources
Links to the Stanford Electronic Humanities Review http://shr.stanford.edu/shreview/

Links to the Humanists Discussion Group http://www.princeton.edu/
~mccarty/humanist/humanist.html
Links to National Endowment for the Humanities http://ns1.neh.fed.us/
Links to Humanities and Social Sciences Online at Michigan State
University http://h-net2.msu.edu/
    with a link to Humanities Online Citation Guide by Melvin E. Page for
History and the Humanities http://h-net2.msu.edu/~africa/citation.html
    with a link to e-mail list of lists http://h-net2.msu.edu/lists/

——wax Web, interactive novel at Univ. of Virginia
http://bug.village.virginia.edu/
****

Scott Rettberg's Books in Chains
http://www.uc.edu/~RETTBESR/links.html
An excellent and comprehensive site that includes information about
resources on the Net.
Links to Bonfire of Liberties, an interactive history of censorship in the
Humanities
http://www.humanities-interactive.org/

FOR FURTHER READING

Clark, Michael. *Cultural Treasures of the Internet.* Upper Saddle River, NJ:
    Prentice-Hall, 1995.
December, John, and Neil Randall. *The World Wide Web Unleashed.* 2nd ed.
    Indianapolis: Sams, 1995.
Dern, Daniel P. *The Internet Guide for New Users.* New York: McGraw-Hill,
    1994.
"Digital Libraries." *Communications of the ACM.* Special Issue. 38.4 (April
    1995).
"Digital Libraries." *SIGLINK Newsletter.* Special Issue. Sep. 1995.
Fahey, Tom. *Net.Speak: The Internet Dictionary.* Indianapolis: Hayden Books,
    1994.
"General Resources on the World Wide Web." *The Arts: Landscape of Our Time.*
    Phi Theta Kappa Honors Study Topic Program Guide, 1996–97.
Grusky, Scott. "Winning Resume." *Internet World* Feb. 1996: 58+.
Hahn, Harley, and Rick Stout. *The Internet YellowPages.* Berkeley: Osborne,
    1994.

Kehoe, Brendan P. *Zen and the Art of the Internet*. 3rd ed. Englewood Cliffs, NJ: Prentice-Hall, 1994.

O'Keefe, Steve. "Electric Text." *Internet World* Oct. 1995: 56+.

"On the Internet." *ACM SIGLINK Newsletter* 4.1 (Mar. 1995): 31+.

Sachs, David, and Henry Stair. *Hands-On Internet: A Beginning Guide for PC Users*. Englewood Cliffs, NJ: Prentice-Hall, 1994.

Sanchez, Robert. "The Digital Press." *Internet World* Sep. 1995, 58–60.

Shea, Virgina. *Netetiquette*. San Francisco: Albion Books, 1994.

Vincent, Patrick. *Free Stuff from the World Wide Web*. Scottsdale: Coriolis Group, 1995.

CHAPTER FIVE

Correspondence & Chat

Background
E-Mail
Chat
MUD/MOO

> *Much of the confusion of our present age stems intrinsically from the divergent experiences of Western literate man, on the one hand, and his new surround of simultaneous or acoustic knowledge, on the other hand. Western man is torn between the claims of visual and auditory cultures or structures.*
>
> THE GLOBAL VILLAGE

BACKGROUND

In the early days of the Internet, computers were first linked together as computer networks through a common operating environment called UNIX. Pioneering Internet users exchanged information through a system of electronic packets (TCP/IP) that bundled messages for an electronic mail system (e-mail). There are two technical names for the types of message bundling: **synchronous** and **asynchronous.** A synchronous transmission means that the message is taking place as it is sent, like real-time chat. Asynchronous means that a message is sent and reassembled into its correct order, like e-mail.

With the introduction of see-it-now word-processing capabilities to select and change font style, add graphics, colors, and backgrounds, Netscape Communicator and Internet Explorer enable users to send either plain text messages or Web pages. As a result of the sophistication of electronic correspondence, writing style and the level of formality suited to the purpose of the message now command a new role in written expression. More importantly, because digital written expression is both a medium of self-expression and the preferred mode of group exchange throughout the Web, understanding how to create effective messages that generate appropriate responses is imperative.

E-MAIL

E-mail Account

A user must have an e-mail account with a provider to be able to send and receive e-mail. The e-mail address of an individual consists of the user's unique account name and Internet provider's server address.

$$\text{hawkes@dal.devry.edu}$$

Acct. Name	Server Path	Top-Level Domain Name

Format

Most Web browsers include an e-mail form that acts as a **template** to ensure the accuracy of addressing e-mail. Figure 5.1 shows the form for the Navigator (Communicator) browser with a draft of a student's description. E-mail mixes elements of traditional letters and memos and contains four parts:

- Heading information
- Message
- Opening and closing
- Signature

Heading Information.   If a software program accomplishes only one task it is called a **dedicated software program.** Dedicated e-mail software pro-

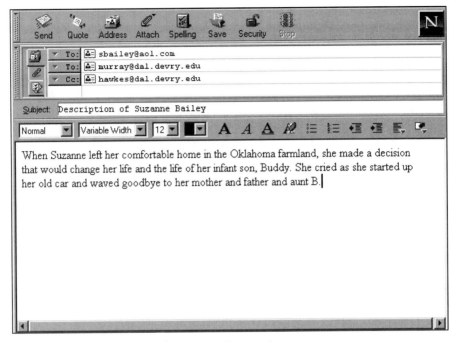

FIGURE 5.1 *E-mail Template for Netscape Communicator*

grams like Eudora™ and the new browsers prompt e-mail authors to fill out
a form for heading information which follows this memorandum format:

To: Recipient's e-mail address
Cc: Other recipient e-mail address
Bc: Copy sent to recipient without disclosing the e-mail address
Subject: Noun phrase that summarizes the contents of the e-mail

When the e-mail is sent, the browser adds the sender's e-mail address as a
From: element and the sending date and time from the computer's operating
clock. Multiple recipients can receive the same e-mail message if each e-mail
account name is separated from others by a comma, like this:

To: sbailey@aol.com, murray@dal.devry.edu

The same is true for multiple recipients in the copy (Cc) or blind copy (Bc)
option. The new browsers automatically enter an account name on a separate
line in the form when they detect a comma to separate account names. In
addition, groups of e-mail account names can be saved to a plain text file and

then cut and pasted into an e-mail form. New versions of Internet Explorer and Netscape Navigator permit users to save names, addresses, phone numbers, etc., along with e-mail account names.

Because busy people screen e-mail two ways, the Subject line is essential. First, a recipient scans the e-mail list on the basis of the sender's name and the importance of the sender to the recipient. Second, a recipient surveys the topical content on the basis of the subjects of the e-mail messages. Often there is a **thread** or a series of messages on the same subject. New browsers also note a reference number to indicate the sequence in which the message was received according to the thread. For example, the third message in a series of messages dealing with the subject Privacy Laws would have a 3 appearing in the heading information. A good Subject line summarizes the contents of the e-mail fairly and accurately. In newsgroups the Subject line helps the owner correctly index the message.

Message.   The message of an e-mail correspondence should quickly convey the author's central idea. Logical order and coherent expression always promote the author's credibility. Naturally, the formality of the message determines the writing style. For example, a message written to the president of the United States warrants a formal style with third person narrative, dignified language, and very respectful tone, while a message written to an old friend would be informal and written in first person or second person narrative, and might include contractions and slang expressions. A report sent to a business associate would have a concise business style, while an essay transmitted to a recreational newsgroup concerned with sports heroes might have a conversational style and perhaps some jargon, too. Standard grammar, punctuation, and paragraph breaks are essential to provide clarity and to connect logical thoughts.

Paragraphs can be indented or flush left with a clear line to separate blocks of text. Lines, bullets, and special characters are used sparingly. Because e-mail is transmitted as **ASCII text,** it has a uniform appearance that uses common keyboard characters. Generally, the same standards for capitalization and punctuation in print-based expression apply to e-mail. Proper nouns, titles, and surnames are capitalized. However, a message in all capital letters denotes shouting and is considered tacky and arrogant. New browsers also allow colored text to distinguish headings, to group paragraphs together into topical areas, and to indicate quoted information.

Because e-mail is an emerging publishing medium, rules for punctuation may vary from traditional usage. Typically, the dash or the colon show a continuation of thought, a comma divides simple enumerations, and a semicolon divides complex enumerations with internal punctuation. Sentences end with a period or a question mark and may include special characters or acronyms like BTW (by the way) or emoticons like :-) for a smile. Much like conversation, e-mail can be spontaneous, using the present tense and active voice. Surprisingly, there are few transitional phrases or carefully selected figures of speech. Although misspelling and faulty punctuation may be tolerated to a degree because of the spontaneous nature of the composition, people judge you by what you say and how you say it. Their perception of you as a credible author may be affected by the errors they see in your work.

Of course, tolerance for style and grammar errors does not extend to poor choices in vocabulary that produce language that is inflammatory, discourteous, threatening, or vulgar. Jargon and shoptalk may be appreciated by those who understand it, but bureaucratic language, double-talk, name-calling, and graphical depictions of insulting gestures are seldom welcome. Many Internet providers have adopted rules of conduct to regulate profanity and threatening language. Within corporations, e-mail is considered company property and may be read by company officials. Lawyers have successfully subpoenaed e-mail records, which have been valuable evidence for convictions in fraud and criminal negligence cases. Federal agencies have tracked down e-mail users who have threatened federal officials and their family members or who have misrepresented themselves for criminal gain, or who have used the system to coerce others into wrongful acts. Currently, there is a growing number of stalker cases in which individuals who pursue others relentlessly through e-mail are being prosecuted and sentenced in criminal courts.

In an effort to avoid misunderstandings in written expression, e-mail authors establish a visual and verbal context for their messages by combining language and symbols to convey emotion and emphasis. Unfortunately, e-mail is judged quickly and at face value. As a product of human invention and organization, the language of an e-mail message may seem innocent enough to the author, but can be misconstrued if the language is ambiguous or the point is contentious. For reasons of brevity and uniformity, an e-mail message may include **acronyms** for common conversational expressions, typographical characters to enclose a word or a phrase that indicate a reaction or significance, and standard keyboard characters to make a **smiley** to denote an emotion. In Figure 5.2, acronyms, characters, and smileys are explained in relation to their meanings. A few example sentences show how to combine these elements to produce a readable message.

In addition to visual elements of acronyms and symbols, some conversation within e-mail messages, chat rooms, and similar forums use stage directions in angle brackets to signify a mood and make clear an author's intentions. These visual shortcuts are:

		Characters		**Smileys**	
Expression	*Acronym*	*Symbol*	*Meaning*	☺	*Emotion*
BCNU	Be seeing you	*	Bold	:-]	Bored
BTW	By the way	_	Underscore	8:)	Bowhead
CFP	Call for papers	< >	Reaction	:-)	Happy
FYI	For your information	>	Quoted	[:|]	Robot
IMHO	In my humble opinion	CAP	SHOUT	:-(	Sad
RFC	Request for comments	Example: TTFN and keep in touch. :-)			
RTFM	Read the fascinating manual	Example: IMHO I think he's cute <sigh>.			
TIA	Thanks in advance	Example: FYI the title is _Cold Fire_.			
TTFN	Ta ta for now	Example: In the CFP the deadline is today.			

FIGURE 5.2 *Acronyms and Symbols*

<cheer>	<shout>
<cry>	<sigh>
<grin> or <g>	<slap>
<hug>	<waves>
<kiss>	<whisper>
<moan>	<yawns>

Unique to e-mail is the opportunity to merge more than one person's text into a message. E-mail software allows for collaboration among recipients who can break up an original message into parts and then respond to those parts. Usually, the quoted material from another source is indented or shown with a symbol like an angle bracket > preceding each quoted line. Offering an exciting opportunity for students to add commentary to one another's work, e-mail is a viable way for classmates to undertake peer reviews of essays.

Here is an example of an e-mail commentary that inserts both directive and evaluative comments into the essay of a classmate (note the use of a different typeface to distinguish the commentary from the text):

> > Music seems to have never been *only* music. For cen-
> >turies cultures have used music in various forms of heal-
> >ing. Priests used chants to heal in ancient Greece, India,
> >China, and Egypt. In the European medieval period, in
> >order to

Directive	**Change "In the European medieval period" to "During the European . . ."**
	>analyze pulse rhythms, physicians were required to study >music (Gardner 92).
Evaluative	**I wonder if another might be to reorganize your examples in historical order rather than going from the medieval period forward to the American settlement and back to the Greek culture.**
	>Native Americans applied specific songs to different ill->nesses. The Greeks used music to treat insomnia, anxiety, >and poor digestion (Strauss 48). Many other cultures have >been using music in healing for hundreds of years.

Opening and Closing.   An e-mail message may start with an opening or salutation. The form of the salutation depends on the relationship of the sender to the receiver. If the recipient is a business associate or an acquaintance, this form of salutation precedes the message

Marvin—
or
Hello Marvin,

If the recipient is unknown or a stranger, the form of salutation should match your knowledge about the recipient

Hello:
Hello Dr. Harper:

A closing indicates that an e-mail message is finished. Again, the level of familiarity dictates the content of the closing. Typical closings for business associates are

Regards,
Cheers,
Best regards,

Closings for friends will vary depending on the closeness of the relationship. However, because e-mail messages are transferable to strangers, you should be careful how you begin and end your messages.

Signature.   Mentioned in Chapter 3, the signature validates the content of the message, provides information about contacting the sender, and may give a hint of the sender's personality in any slogan that may be added.

Sender's Name
Sender's Title, Organization
Voice:
FAX:
E-mail:
Proverb or saying

New browsers help the sender to design and store in memory a signature that is quickly recalled and placed in the message as a signature file. As a quick reference, Figure 5.3 compares the level of acquaintance with the appropriate form of expression in the salutation, closing and signature.

Attachments.   Occasionally, there is a need for additional materials that are too distracting or too cumbersome to include in an e-mail message. Text files, sound files, and video clips are just a few of the files that can be electronically appended to an e-mail and sent as an **attachment.** New developments in word-processing software mean that word-processed documents

Relationship	Salutation	Closing	Signature
Stranger	Hello: Hello Name:	Regards	Your full name, title, and e-mail address (with optional voice and fax listings) Ex: Bill Clinton, President president@whitehouse.gov
Acquaintance	First name only: First name,	Regards, Cheers,	Your full name, title, and e-mail address (with optional voice and fax listings)
Friend or well-known acquaintance	First name only,	None or one suited to the closeness of the relationship and the nature of the message	Your full name, e-mail address, (with optional voice and fax listings), and a thought-provoking expression _____ Ex: Bill Clinton, President president@whitehouse.gov —— building bridges to the 21st century

FIGURE 5.3 *Customary Expressions in E-mail*

can also be sent as e-mail with the .doc (Microsoft Word) extension. In either Internet Explorer or Netscape Communicator, a user can select the Attach button and then browse a list of files on the computer to finally select the one (or more) to include. Text from a word-processed document can be embedded in an e-mail message by cutting it from the document and pasting it as part of the text of an e-mail.

TRAVEL ADVISORY: Protocol for Successful E-mail

1. Be careful what you write or illustrate. Your message is in print and can be passed on without your permission.
2. Be careful to whom you send copies. Some messages are not meant to be passed on to colleagues or superiors without the permission of the author.
3. Be concise and economical in your e-mail messages by stating your requests for information clearly toward the beginning of the message and indicating the purpose of the e-mail in the subject line.
4. Threats, abusive language, harassment, and pornography are punishable by local, state, and federal laws even though the incident appears in electronic form.
5. Your e-mail is not private. Corporations have successfully searched e-mail files to find supporting evidence in court cases. Simply because you delete your e-mail does not mean that it does not still exist on the server in some form.
6. Although there is a tolerance for style and grammar errors because of the spontaneous nature of e-mail, people get a sense of who you are by the way you express yourself.
7. If you think you need to keep a copy of your e-mail for your records, print it out and save it to a floppy disk that you keep to archive important messages. Some e-mail services automatically delete week-old messages.

IRC Chat

Internet Relay Chat (IRC) began in 1988 in Finland when Jarkko Oikarinen was trying to improve the **Bulletin Board System (BBS),** which was an early text-based method of giving and receiving files and messages online. He experimented with components and read technical papers to devise a way to carry typed messages on channels to multiple users. Although the technique was revolutionary, it took some time for the rest of the world to discover how to apply it. IRC makes spontaneous conversation possible for online guest lectures or class discussion. Capitalizing on the IRC potential, **Multi-User Dungeon (MUD)** and **MUD Object Oriented (MOO)** are virtual environments in which people engage in conversation or find a way through a maze of objects and pathways. In addition, both Internet Explorer and Netscape Navigator offer a suite of applications including conferencing software that permits multiple sites to share real-time exchanges. Both browsers facilitate explanation with a whiteboard or a graphics tablet that allows users to draw examples as though they were in a classroom.

IRC is running on 60 server sites in the United States. Because IRC responds to requests from other servers all over the world, it is called a **server-client system** (Harris 6). For example, a Web server at New Mexico State University sends a request to the IRC server at Northwestern University in Illinois to open channels for real-time communication. The IRC server responds with a list of publicly available channels and allows the users at New Mexico State University to select and interact with the users on any of the channels. Figure 5.4 shows a channel arrangement.

Although the technical interaction of servers make connection to a chat appear seamless, to take part in a chat-oriented Web site (Figure 5.5), a user must supply an e-mail address, select a unique alias and password, and find an area of the chat to enter. Typically, the chat is subdivided into rooms with names to carry out the overall theme of the chat along with a posted capacity for each room. In each room there is a moderator who can be a person or a computer program acting as an announcer. Not only does the moderator keep a count of the participants in each room, the moderator also announces when someone has entered or left the room. For a special occasion like the guest participation of a famous person, a chat area can have a **facilitated chat** in which a human moderator accepts or even screens questions before passing them on to the guest celebrity. Chats permit a user to log the entire contents of the session, to ignore outside messages, to send an immediate message

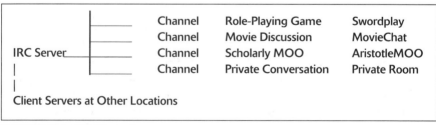

FIGURE 5.4 *IRC Channels*

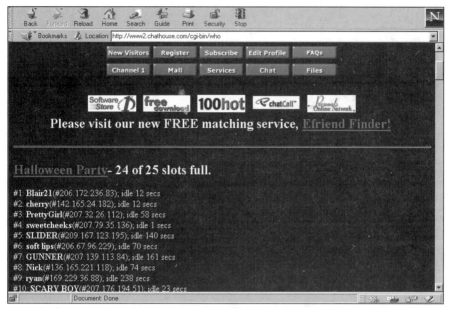

FIGURE 5.5 *Chat Area Options. Reprinted, by permission, from the Channel 1 Chathouse.*

to any participant, or even to send a secret message to any participant by highlighting that person's alias on the list of chat room guests. Infrequently, the moderator of the chat will summon a user into a private area to advise that person about the rules of the chat. Figure 5.6 lists frequently used commands for chat rooms.

As seen in Figure 5.5 a chat menu displays an array of hot buttons to acquaint users with the site's purpose and rules, followed by an announcement of a new participant entering the room. Later, dialogue boxes appear so that chat may continue. In these dialogue boxes, conversations take place and are written in informal style, which can incorporate smileys like :-) , emotions like <sigh>, abbreviated expressions like BTW, and even animated figures like four dancing skeletons or a playful cat. Users' conversations range from small talk to philosophical discussions. Expression can be light-hearted or dramatic. Just like face-to-face encounters, crosstalk can prove distracting, so participants must concentrate to keep track of what is being said. Participants in the chat area may or may not talk to a newcomer. A good way to enter the conversation is to ask a question or agree to a previous statement. Figure 5.7 illustrates the arrangement of dialogue boxes.

Command	Description	Typical Function
/join #room	Attempts to enter the chatroom.	Used in conjunction with a password.
/nick	Establishes a nickname following the command.	Name sets your nickname/personality.
/whois	Reveals the identity of the person named after the command.	Whois lists data about the nickname.
/topic	Sets the discussion topic of the chat room.	You may not have authority to do so.
/ignore name	Hides messages from the person named after the command.	Essentially refuses messages from the person named.
/quit	Exits chat room.	Ends chat session.

FIGURE 5.6 *Common Chat Room Commands*

When researching a subject area, chat area discussions can be found through a query to a search engine or by contacting a Web page that links to several chats. Engaging in chat can lead to a new perspective through group collaboration on a topic, or it can anonymously test a belief or stance in order to prepare a stronger argument. Without the pretensions of name and title, users tend to react honestly when asked for an opinion. Depending on the chat area, there is also a tolerance for not-so-perfect written expression, which provides an opportunity for someone learning English to practice in the vernacular.

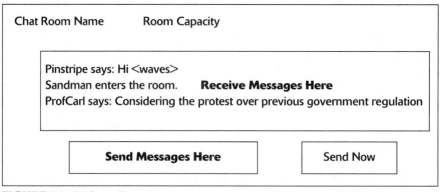

FIGURE 5.7 *Dialogue Boxes*

SHORTLIST 21
Chat Rooms/IRC Information

Public Access Chat Rooms
http://www.chatcom.com/

Chat House
http://www.chathouse.com/

IRC Intro
http://www.mirc.co.uk/ircintro.html

Multi-User Dungeon (MUD) and MUD Object Oriented (MOO)

A sense of play pervades the Web and the evolution of the MUD is a case in point. Predating the Finnish creation of IRC by a decade, English programmers Richard Bartle and Roy Trubshaw wrote the first MUD program to enable players to interact in a text-based adventure game. By joining a MUD, a user adopts a character's role and thereby a character's name as an alias. A MUD server may offer a list of possible characters or let the user make up a character and the character's attributes. Like a chat, actions and expression can be monitored by a human or program-driven moderator. Unlike the chat in which the user is stationary, the MUD requires command-driven movement (Figure 5.8) and action that may be awkward at first.

From the MUD, came a MOO, and a **MUSH (Multiuser Shared Hallucination)** that had three major differences. First, players are not in a competition to get somewhere or find something or even behave like the character they have assumed. Second, participants are cotravelers in virtual space and share observations as well as misgivings. The point of a MOO is not to hurry

2nd floor library

You have just entered the library through the huge oak door. To the North is a small table with the bust of Socrates on it, to the East is a stained glass window behind an antique mahogany desk, to the South is a wall of oil paintings and on the floor in front of you is a trap door. You hear a loud, shrill laugh behind you. You turn and no one is there.
>

FIGURE 5.8 *Command-Driven Movement*

SHORTLIST 22
MUD/MOO Sites

Adventus (based on fantasy themes)
http://cslib.ecs.soton.ac.uk/~cslmud

Elendor MUSH (J.R.R. Tolkein)
http://where.com/Elendor/Welcome.html

Cumulative list of MUDs
http://www.absi.com/mud/mud.html

MUD FAQ
http://www.math.okstate.edu/~jds/mudfaqp1.html

MUD Resource Page
http://www.cis.upenn.edu/~lal/mudinfo.html

MOO/MU Document Library
http://lucien.berkeley.edu/moo.html

through all the virtual spaces, but to linger a while and get to know cotravelers by writing reactions to colors, clutter, and animated objects. Third, participation in a MOO, whether it is the Hypertext Hotel or The Sprawl, suspends users in a world of chaotic text from which they have to determine important points of interest and pathways to take. Not only are researchers and composition teachers interested in building MOOs as creative means to involve students in their own writing processes, but MOOs are also becoming a springboard for programmers involved in **Virtual Reality Markup Language (VRML)** and **Object Oriented Programming (OOP).** These programmers seem to be keenly aware of the exciting aspect of building a true hypertextual universe of words and images suspended in cyberspace. Chapter 10 examines vitual reality sites.

TRAVEL ADVISORY: Protocol for Chat, MUD, MOO

1. Read all introductory material to understand the purpose of the site.
2. If the site requires more than your e-mail address to enter, decide whether you will divulge further information or be willing to pay a fee for the service.
3. Copy down the Web administrator's e-mail address for future reference.

4. When you are asked to pick a nickname or alias, pick a name that you would be comfortable with and a password that is different from your alias, but easily remembered.

5. Be aware that an alias is a freely chosen pseudonym. Anyone can impersonate. Males can have female aliases; females can have male aliases; some aliases are non-descriptive like "pinstripe" and other aliases are overly descriptive like the "love doctor." Aliases can be an indicator of expectation and personal interests.

6. Obey the rules of the area. If you are offended, report the incident.

7. Carrying on an exchange in a private area may put newer users at risks. Always remember you have the right to leave the area, to report violations to the site owner, and to simply turn off your computer.

Through the Looking Glass

The following exercises allow you to explore and draw conclusions about what you see; in essence, you get to be the expert.

WEB LINGO

acronyms	Multi-User Dungeon (MUD)
ASCII text	Multiuser Shared Hallucination (MUSH)
asynchronous	Object Oriented Programming (OOP)
attachment	smiley
Bulletin Board System (BBS)	synchronous
dedicated software program	template
facilitated chat	thread
Internal Relay Chat (IRC)	Virtual Reality Markup Language (VRML)
MUD Object Oriented (MOO)	

TRAVEL TIP: Address Book

Establish a writing network by sending e-mail to your classmates by using the Address Book to store names and e-mail addresses.

For the Netscape
Address Book

1. Select the Communicator option from the Menu bar at the top of the browser's screen.
2. Select Address Book.
3. From the options at the top of the Address Book menu, select New Card. Fill out the information form.

For the Internet
Explorer Address Book

1. Select the Go option from the menu of options at the top of the browser.
2. You may click on the New Contact icon or the New Group icon.
3. In a dialog box, enter the first, last and middle name as well as e-mail address(es) and other pertinent information.

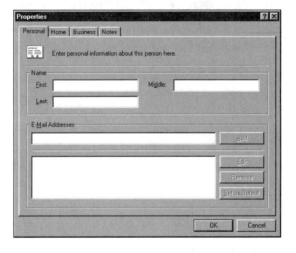

Both browsers permit editing Address Book entries by left clicking on the entry in the list of addresses in the Address Book and then displaying the entry's Properties information by right clicking.

WEB ITINERARY

1. Interview a classmate and write a description of the classmate as an e-mail message sent to the entire class. Have others in the class correct the description to be more accurate.

2. The "Pioneers of Computing" page located in Virtual Web Museum of Computing (http://www.comlab.ox.ac.uk/archive/other/museums/computing/pioneers.html) contains a list of outstanding leaders in Internet development. Find three leaders currently active in shaping Internet ventures. Use the search engine Hot Bot at http://www.hotbot.com to find the e-mail addresses of these famous people. Write a short description of who they are and add them to your Address Book. Examples are:

   Esther Dyson, Information Technologist
   Michael Eisner, Disney CEO
   Bill Gates, Microsoft CEO
   Marvin Minsky, Cognitive Scientist
   Jakob Nielsen, Information Designer
   Bruce Sterling, Science Fiction Author

3. Visit a chat room. Write a site report in which you describe your visit to a chat room, the purpose of the site, the rules of conduct, and an evaluation of your experience. Send the site report to your classmates with a copy to your instructor.

4. MOOs and MUDs join imagination with expression to create a virtual world. Given the controversy over role-playing games and their influence on Internet users, compose a persuasive essay that identifies problems associated with role-playing games, your judgment about the significance of the problems, and your proposed solution to the problems that you have presented. Send a copy of the essay to a trusted classmate for review and editing. Post this essay to a discussion list.

PROJECT ASSIGNMENT

Collaboration and peer review are excellent ways to improve writing. Using a brainstorming session either in class or through an IRC connection, develop a list of issues confronting higher education. Elect a facilitator who will manage the project. Assign one issue to each member of the class, who then researches the issue, writes an informative article about it, and e-mails the completed article to the managing editor. The editor then copies and pastes the contributed articles in an e-mail–based newsletter using the enhanced graphics and color features of the new browsers. The newsletter should include the following components:

- A masthead with the title of the newsletter, issuing group, and date of publication.

- A table of contents in the sequence of the topics discussed.
- Banner headings to set off each topic.
- At the end, an identification of the managing editor, a list of contributors, a statement about how the information can be used and by whom, a date of creation, and an e-mail address for users to send feedback.

CHAPTER SIX
Search Finds

> *As voice, print, image, and sensory data proceed simultaneously, figure and ground are often in apposition rather than in a sequential relationship. For example, the consciousness of the data-base user is in two places at once: at the terminal and in the center of the system.*
>
> THE GLOBAL VILLAGE

SEARCH ENGINES

A search engine is a software program that roams the Internet to gather information that matches a search statement entered by the user. Guided by the user's search statement, the search engine accesses huge numbers of files quickly, returning a list of probable sites with a brief description of each one extracted from the contents of the home pages and supplying a clickable hypertext link to the site's URL. Figure 6.1 depicts this process.

Often called webcrawler or webworm programs, these search engine programs instantly compare the user's search statement to Web documents' titles, seek matching words in the Web page contents, inspect the combination

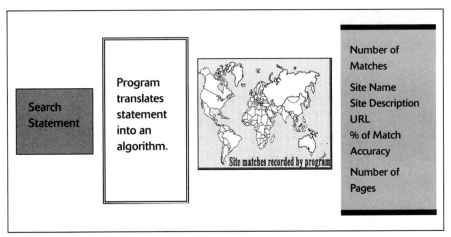

FIGURE 6.1 *Search Engine Process*

of characters in the URL, and follow corresponding links to other documents at other sites in order to perform the same function over again and again.

The Web, however, is not the originator of the search engine. As noted earlier, Archie, named after the cartoon character, was a program developed to crawl through ftp sites and find matches to keywords in the user's search statements. Unfortunately, Archie had two drawbacks. The search for information was limited to subject areas, and the search process itself required a programmer's command of the UNIX operating system. As a user-friendly refinement on Archie, the Veronica program operated as an interface to search gopher sites by titles. Saving users from labor-intensive coding of search statements, the Veronica program crawled through gopher sites to return a list of sites. Still, the list of sites generated by Veronica was not comprehensive.

Offering both comprehensive inquiry and user-friendly interfaces, two kinds of search sites for the Web are a **metasearch engine** and a **dedicated search engine**. The first kind is a search engine that concurrently examines data held by other search engines to find requested information. For example, in the metasearch SavvySearch engine (Figure 6.2), a user can enter a search statement and the engine will simultaneously access a wide array of resources or a more narrow set of resources, depending on the choice indicated in a check box. Helpful in beginning searches into a subject area, metasearch engines cut down the length of time needed to gather a list of sites that provide information matching a search statement.

Popular independent metasearch engines are listed in Figure 6.3. These search engines handle a high volume of traffic daily, supplying current information that is well organized, attractively arranged, and easy to use. With

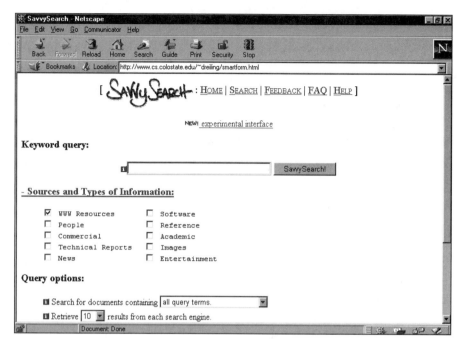

FIGURE 6.2 *SavvySearch. Reprinted, by permission, from Daniel Dreilinger.*

the enormous amount of information accumulating on the Web and the search process being an integral part of finding information quickly, a new kind of advisory site, listed in Shortlist 23, has appeared that gives how-to advice on formulating an efficient search statement suited to specific search engines. Developed for San Diego State University, Bruce Harley's recommended WWW sites give users accurate and clear advice to customize search statements for Yahoo, InfoSeek, AltaVista, and metasearch engines. Located at DeVry New Brunswick, Bhupinder Sran's Online Search Seminar provides tips and techniques for online searching based on research for his dissertation. HyperNews is an extensive collection of search techniques, advice, and useful links.

Site Name	Uniform Resource Locator
All-in-One	http://www.albany.net/allinone/index.html
MetaCrawler	http://search5.metacrawler.com/home.html
SavvySearch	http://www.cs.colostate.edu/~dreiling/smartform.html
W3 Search Engines	http://cuiwww.unige.ch/meta-index.html

FIGURE 6.3 *Popular Metasearch Indexes*

SHORTLIST 23
Search Engine Advisory

HyperNews
http://union.ncsa.uiuc.edu/HyperNews/get/www/searching.html

Online Search Seminar
http://www.admin.nj.devry.edu/~bsran/onlne_search_seminar_technical_version/

Recommended WWW Search Sites
http://libweb.sdsu.edu/gov/recommend.html

High-quality dedicated search engines with extensive databases have emerged whose maintenance and technical sophistication are possible because of the engine's sponsoring organizations. Independent search engines offer unparalleled research opportunities to the public. Veteran Web researchers may prefer one over another for the type of search that is possible or for the user-friendly structure of the site. For instance, Digital Corporation sponsors AltaVista, which boasts simple and advanced queries that extend to its database containing millions of Web pages and the full contents of more than 13,000 newsgroups (Berkeley). Hailed by C/net as the individual search engine with the "most powerful search capabilities" for its versatility and its adaptability to a novice or an expert's search statements (1996 C/net survey), AltaVista roams the Web to find relevant material in Web pages and within Usenet newsgroups. On the returned list of matching URLs, the engine supplies document summaries. Commended for its two levels of query, AltaVista (Figure 6.4) affords simple and advanced search options. The advanced search options include wildcards, include/exclude options, and logical operators (and, or, not) to narrow the search statement. Moreover, it provides a help tutorial for Advanced Queries that guides seasoned users to more time-efficient use of the engine.

WebCrawler (Figure 6.5) was originally developed by Washington University's Brian Pinkerton and provides a base of 100,000 documents (Winship) and returns matching URLs along with a link to similar pages.

Lycos, developed by Carnegie Mellon University, is preferred by researchers who like its process of determining the percent of relevancy of sites and then ranking likely sites based on their relevancy. Whereas AltaVista searches full text contents, Lycos searches its two databases of URLs and abstracts of the sites to determine matches to user-defined search statements. Lycos is revised on a weekly basis and provides fairly detailed summaries of sites. Recently undergoing a face-lift, perhaps in part due to its partnership

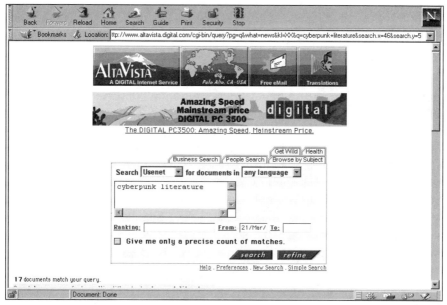

FIGURE 6.4 *AltaVista Search Engine. Reprinted, by permission, from Digital Equipment Corporation. AltaVista, the AltaVista logo, and the Digital logo are trademarks of Digital Equipment Corporation.*

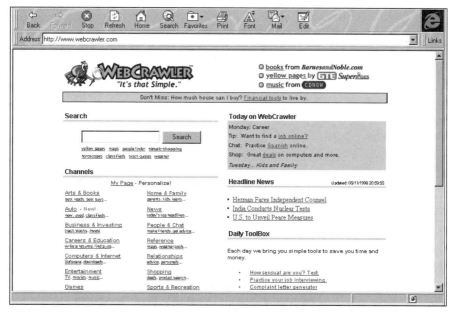

FIGURE 6.5 *WebCrawler Search Engine. Reprinted, by permission, from Excite, Inc. Excite, WebCrawler, and the WebCrawler logo are trademarks of Excite., Inc. and may be registered in various jurisdictions (Excite screen display copyright 1995–1998, Excite, Inc.).*

with Microsoft Corporation, Lycos offers search capabilities, quick references, and subject indexes.

Yahoo, designed and implemented by Stanford University, is now a totally commercial operation. The oldest Web-based search engine, Yahoo searches URLs, Web page titles and contents, and provides a list of categories called a knowledge tree that in turn offers the user the ability to search a subject area, refining and narrowing the scope of the search.

Varying in scope of design and operation, each program directs the acquisition of information and seeks out data in a slightly different manner than other programs, so search engines may gather different data. Figure 6.6 lists popular dedicated search engines. While the search engine advisory in Shortlist 23 has sites for helpful information about how to conduct Internet research, Shortlist 24 lists sites that evaluate search engines.

As you grow more skilled in the electronic research process, you will begin to keep a list of your favorite search engines. Research strategy, however, involves more than finding a list of sites. You will need to evaluate the quality and credi-

Site Name	Uniform Resource Locator
AltaVista	http://altavista.digital.com/
Excite	http://www.excite.com/
HotBot	http://www.hotbot.com/
InfoSeek	http://www.infoseek.com
Lycos	http://www.lycos.com
WebCrawler	http://www.webcrawler.com/
Yahoo	http://www.yahoo.com/

FIGURE 6.6 *Popular Dedicated Search Engines*

SHORTLIST 24
Comparison of Search Engines

Ian R. Winship's WWW Searching Tools—An Evaluation
http://link.bubl.ac.uk:80/search.htm

Digital Library SunSITE's Internet Search Tools Details
http://sunsite.berkeley.edu/Help/searchdetails.html

Cnet's Features Comparison: Individual Search Engines
http://www.cnet.com/Content/Reviews/Compare/Search/ss3a.html

bility of the information (as Chapter 1 suggests) and give proper credit to the sources you use by following electronic documentation guidelines.

DOCUMENTATION

The Modern Language Association (MLA) has guidelines for citing books, periodicals, documents, performances, presentations, artwork, interviews, database files, and software (Figure 6.7). In response to a growing demand for citation guidelines for electronic sources, the MLA has recently revised its guidelines to include electronic documentation on its Web site at http://www.mla.org/main_stl.htm. Other formats include Andrew Harnack and Gene Kleppinger of Eastern Kentucky University's Web site at http://falcon

---

1 Name of author, editor, compiler, or translator of the source (if available and relevant), reversed for alphabetizing and followed by an abbreviation, such as *ed.* if appropriate

2. Title of a poem, short story, article, or similar short work within a scholarly project, database, or periodical (in quotation marks); or title of a posting to a discussion list or forum (taken from the subject line and put in quotation marks), followed by the description *Online posting*

3. Title of a book (underlined)

4. Name of the editor, compiler, or translator of the text (if relevant and if not cited earlier), preceded by the appropriate abbreviation, such as *Ed.*

5. Publication information for any print version of the source

6. Title of the scholarly project, database, periodical, or professional or personal site (underlined); or, for a professional or personal site with no title, a description such as *Home page*

7. Name of the scholarly project or database (if available)

8 Version number of the source (if not part of the title) or, for a journal, the volume number, issue number, or other identifying number

9. Date of electronic publication, of the latest update, or of posting

10. For a posting to a discussion list or forum, the name of the list or forum

11. The number range or total number of pages, paragraphs, or other sections, if they are numbered

12. Name of any institution or organization sponsoring or associated with the Web site

13. Date when the researcher accessed the source

14. Electronic address, or URL, of the source (in angle brackets)

FIGURE 6.7 *MLA General Guidelines for Citations for a Work Cited List. Source: MLA Style at http://www.mla.org/main_stl.htm.*

.eku.edu/honors/beyond-mla/#ftp and Janice Walker of the University of South Florida's Web site at http://www.cas.usf.edu/english/walker/mla. html. The MLA examples from their Web site are somewhat limited and may not cover all Internet resources. Always ask your instructors which format they prefer.

Long regarded for its standardization of documentation style for the social sciences, the American Psychological Association (APA) has also published citation examples (Figure 6.8) geared to the Internet on its Web site at http://www.apa.org/journals/webref.html. You can also visit Xia Li and Nancy Crane from the University of Vermont's site at http://www.uvm.edu/~xli/reference/estyles.html. They developed a system of APA documentation for Internet-based resources.

To simplify presentation of the MLA and APA guidelines, which at times vary greatly, this chapter translates them into citation templates, followed by specific examples. Whenever possible, this chapter repeats the citation exam-

---

1. Begin all references with the same information that would be provided for a printed source
2. Web information is then placed at the end of the reference
3. Use "Retrieved from" and the date because documents on the Web may change in content, move, or be removed from a site altogether
4. Cite e-mail in text only as a personal reference, never on the references list since e-mail can be sent by someone else posing as the author
5. Cite Web sites in text only by the URL, not on the references list
6. Whenever a citation ends in a path (URL) statement, no period follows the path statement

---

FIGURE 6.8 *APA General Guidelines for Citations on a Reference List. Source: How to Cite Information from the Internet and the World Wide Web at http://www.apa.org/journals/webref.html.*

SHORTLIST 25
Documentation Style Guides

American Psychological Association
http://www.apa.org/journals/webref.html

Modern Language Association
http://www.mla.org/main_stl.htm

ple from the MLA or APA Web sites. If the general guidelines are not clear or do not explain how to cite the Internet/Web resource, this chapter extends the general guidelines. An asterisk after the MLA or APA designator indicates that the example is an extension.

Published Works (Major and Minor Writing Projects)

Note: If URLs must be continued on a following line of text, the division should occur at the subdirectory level indicated by "/". No extraneous punctuation like a hyphen should be introduced.

Book

MLA　Author. Title. Publication information for any print version of the source. Scholarly project or database. Editor of the scholarly project or database, if available. Name of sponsoring organization for the Web site. Access date <URL>.

Poe, Edgar Allan. The Murders in the Rue Morgue. 1841. Wiretap Classic Library. 3 May 1993. Swedish University Network. 24 Feb. 1996 <http://ftp.sunet.se/ftp/pub/etext/wiretap-classic-library/Poe/rue.poe>.

APA*　Author/editor. (publication date). Title of the work. [Online] Retrieved date from Internet source: path

Poe, E. A. (1841). Murders in the rue morgue. [Online book project]. Retrieved February 24, 1996 from FTP: ftp.sunet.se/ftp/pub/etext/wiretap-classic-library /Poe/rue.poe

Journal

MLA　Author. "Title." Publication information for any print version of the source including volume number and issue number. Number range or total number of pages, paragraphs, or other sections, if numbered. Access date <URL>.

Kierans, Kenneth. "Beyond Deconstruction." Animus 2 (1997): 46 pars. 24 Feb. 1998 <http://www.mun.ca/animus/1997vol2/kierans1.htm>.

APA　Author. (publication date). Title of the article. Journal name, Number range or total number of paragraphs or sections, if numbered. [Online serial]. Retrieved date from Internet source: path

Kierans, K. (1997). Beyond deconstruction. Animus, 2, 46 pars. [Online serial]. Retrieved February 24, 1996 from the World Wide Web: http://www.mun.ca /animus/1997vol2/kierans1.htm

Magazine

MLA   Author. "Title." Periodical Title. Publication date. Access date<URL>.
"Zap! How the Year 2000 Bug Will Hurt the Economy." 19 Feb. 1998.
Businessweek Online. 24 Feb. 1998 <http://www.business
week.com /1998/09/b3567001.htm>.

APA   Author. (publication date). Title of the article. Periodical name.
[Online serial] Retrieved date from type of Internet source : path
Zap! How the year 2000 bug will hurt the economy. (1998, February
19). Businessweek online. Retrieved February 24, 1998 from
the World Wide Web: http://www.businessweek.com/1998/09/
b3567001.htm

Reference Database

MLA   "Title." Database Name. Version. Publication date. Sponsoring orga-
nization. Access date <URL>.
"Game Theory." Stanford Encyclopedia of Philosophy. 1996. Stanford
U. 24 Feb. 1998 <http:plato.stanford.edu/entries/game-theory>.

APA*   Title. (publication date). Database name [Online]. Retrieved date
from Internet type of source: path
Game theory. (1996). Stanford encyclopedia of philosophy. [Online
reference]. Retrieved February 24, 1998 from the World Wide Web:
http://www.eb.com:180

Web Sites

Note: If a professional or personal site has no title, a designation like *Home
page* is used.

Scholarly Project

MLA   Author. Title. Publication information for any print version of the
source. Scholarly project or database. Editor of the scholarly project or database, if available. Name of sponsoring organization for
the Web site. Access date <URL>.
Scholarly Communications Project. 2 Feb. 1998. Virginia Polytechnic
Institute. 24 Feb. 1998 <http://scholar.lib.bt.edu/>.

APA   Note: Web sites, as opposed to specific documents, are referenced in
text with the URL; they are not included in the Reference list.

Professional Site (creation date/update added to the MLA example)

MLA*   Site Name. Creation date or update. Sponsoring organization.
Access date <URL>.

Philosophy General Resources. 31 Jan. 1998. Factasia Philosophy Resource Hub. 24 Feb. 1998 <http://cybercom.net/~rbjones/rbipub/philos/inter/015.htm>.

Personal Site (creation date/update added to the MLA example)

MLA Web page author. Site Name. Creation date or update. Access date <URL>.

Hawkes, Lory. Home page. 15 Jan. 1998. 2 Feb. 1998 <http://home pages.waymark.net/~hawkes/index.html>.

Artistic Work

Literature/Poetry/Play/Film/Music

MLA Author. "Work's Title." Publication. Information on print version. Title of Scholarly Project or Database. Project or database editor. Date of electronic publication. Sponsoring organization. Access date <URL>.

Blake, William. "The Shepherd." Songs of Innocence. 1789. William Blake Archive. 12 Feb. 1998. U. of Virginia. 24 Feb. 1998 <http://jefferson.village.edu/blake/main.html>.

APA Note: APA provides no examples.

Graphic Art

Image, background, icon, or graphic element (object) reused from an Internet source (the file name without the extension is the title of the object. For example, cyborg.jpg would be cited as Cyborg.)

MLA* Artist or Designer. "Title." Site Name. Object type. Sponsoring organization. Electronic publication date. Access date <URL>.

Myerson, Barry. "Cyborg." Graphics for Free. Image. Clarity U. 1 Nov. 1997. 4 Nov. 1997 <http://departments.clarity.edu/~myerson/~myerson/index.html/cyborg.jpg>.

Electronic Correspondence (E-mail, IRC, MUD, MOO)

Personal E-Mail Message

MLA Use the subject or title of the e-mail, if known. If this e-mail appears on a public list, use the list citation style. There are separate styles for personal e-mail messages.

In-text reference: (Author date)

Style 1

Author. "Subject." E-mail to author. day Month year.

Houston, Amy. "New Technologies." E-mail to author. 13 Sep. 1997.

Style 2

Author. "Subject." E-mail to author. day Month year.

Carlton, Sam. "Distance Education Issues." E-mail to Jerry Nelson. 4
Apr. 1997.

APA   E-mail correspondence does not appear on a reference list. However,
e-mail is cited within the text.

In-text reference: S. Carlton (personal communication, April 4, 1997)
or (S. Carlton, personal communication, April 4, 1997)

The Author's Listserv Comment

MLA*   Author. "Subject." Online posting. Publication date. List name.
Access date <Listserv's electronic address or URL>.

Abraham, Carolyn. "The Virtual Institute of Information." Online
posting. 29 Jul. 1996. Technology and Education Forum. 1 Aug.
1996 <teched@clarity.edu>.

APA   If the date is unknown, put in the access date. Do not use a period
after the path.

Author/editor. (publication date). Subject of message. Discussion
list name: [Online], xx. Retrieved date from Internet source: path

Abraham, Carolyn. (1996, July 29). The virtual institute of information. Technology and education forum: [Online posting].
Retrieved August 1, 1996 from: teched@clarity.edu.

Listserv Comment

MLA*   Author. "Subject." Online posting. Publication date. List name.
Access date <listserv's electronic address or URL>.

Carlton, Sam. "Distance Education Issues." Online posting. 6 Apr.
1997. Technology and Education Forum. 15 Apr. 1997 <teched
@clarity.edu>.

APA*   Author/editor. (publication date). Subject of message. Discussion
list name: [Online], xx. Retrieved date from Internet source: path

Carlton, S. (1997, April 6). Distance education issues. Technology
and education forum: [Online]. Retrieved April 15, 1997 from:
teched@clarity.edu

Republished Listserv Comment

MLA*   Author. "Subject." Online posting. Original publication date. List
name via Republishing source. Access date <republished list-
serv's electronic address or URL>.

Carlton, Sam. "Distance Education Issues." Online posting. 6 Apr.
1997. Technology and Education Forum via IAT Infobits. 18 Apr.
1997 <iat@mhs.unc.edu>.

APA* Author/editor. (republished publication date). Subject. <u>Republished source</u>: [Online]. Retrieved date from Internet source: republished source's path

Carlton, Sam. (1997, April 6). Distance education issues. <u>IAT infobits</u>: [Online]. Retrieved April 18, 1997 from: iat@mhs.unc.edu

Newsgroup

MLA* Author. "Subject." Online posting. Publication date. Newsgroup Name. Access date <Newsgroup's URL>.

Jarlind, Bob. "Nanotechnology and Microbiology." Online posting. 5 May 1997.alt.science.nanotechnology. 9 Sep. 1997 <nanotechnology @clarity.edu>.

APA* Author. (publication date). Subject. <u>Newsgroup name</u>: [Online]. Retrieved date from Internet source: path

Jarlind, B. (1997, May 5). Nanotechnology and microbiology. <u>Alt. science.nanotechnolgy</u>: [Online]. Retrieved September 9, 1997 from: nanotechnology@clarity.edu

IRC Chat and Other Synchronous Communications (MOOs, MUDs, etc.)

MLA* Author. "Title." Description (group discussion, personal interview, position statements). Date of occurrence. Sponsoring organization. Access date <URL>.

Len Hatfield. "Interview of Stuart Moulthrop by students in English 5334." Group Interview. 18 Apr. 1995. 12 Dec. 1996 <http:// ebbs.english.vt.edu:80/hthl /moulthrop.webchat.html>.

APA APA considers this type of communication personal and references it only in text.

Special Cirumstances

Linked File

A linked file from an individual's and corporation's home page:

MLA* Author. "Title." Publication date. Linked from <u>Site Name</u> at "Source Document." Access date <source document's URL>.

Thompson, Carl. "New Intranet Developments." 30 June 1996. Linked from Netscape at "Intranet." 1 Nov. 1996 <http:// home.netscape.com/intranet/>.

APA* Author/editor. (publication date). Title. <u>Site Name</u>. [Online], xx. Retrieved date via linked file from Internet source: path

Thompson, Carl. (1996, June 30). New intranet developments. <u>Intranet</u>. [Online white paper]. Retrieved November 1, 1996 via <u>Netscape</u> home page from the World Wide Web: http://home. netscape.com/intranet

A linked file from an archive's home page (no author or update apparent):

MLA* Author. "Document Title." Publication date. Linked from Site Name at "Source Document." Access date at <source document's URL>.

"OWL Handouts by Subject." 1 Feb. 1996. Linked from Purdue On-Line Writing Lab at "Table of Contents." 22 Feb. 1996 <http://owl.trc.purdue.edu/toc.html>.

APA* Author/editor. (publication date). Title. Site Name [Online], xx. Retrieved date via linked file from Internet source: path

OWL handouts by subject. (1996, February 1). Purdue On-Line Writing Lab [Online handout]. Retrieved February 22, 1996 via Table of contents from the World Wide Web: http://owl.trc.purdue.edu/toc

Through the Looking Glass

The following exercises allow you to explore and draw conclusions about what you see; in essence, you get to be the expert.

WEB LINGO

dedicated search engine

metasearch engine

WEB ITINERARY

1. Refer to the guidelines in this chapter to document the entire list of sites in Shortlist 22, on page 78, using both MLA and APA style.

2. Using a metasearch engine, investigate the following terms so that you can write a definition about each one: technology transfer, categorical imperative, ethnocentrism, illuminated manuscripts, and visual literacy.

3. Use four or five dedicated search engines to find information on an obscure topic. Write an evaluation report in which you compare the search engines for ease of use, features, and performance.

4. Compile a bibliography of electronic sources dealing with the Renaissance. Arrange the sites in a knowledge tree with categories like architecture, art, history, literature, poetry.
5. Compile a bibliography of electronic sources dealing with the history and issues of electronic commerce.

TRAVEL TIP: Transforming the Discovery Journal into a Bookmark List

Make your discovery journal into a hypertext document so that your URLs become hypertext links to the sites and function as an annotated bookmark list. There are three hypertext markup language codes that you need to know:

 	Break; functions as a carriage return
<p>	Paragraph; functions as a double space
<a href="URL">title</a>	Link; enables a jump to the named URL

For either Netscape or Internet Explorer

1. Open Notepad or WordPad from the Windows 95 Accessories Group.
2. Open the text file that holds your discovery journal.
3. With the text file displayed, add the codes to put in spacing and links.
4. Use the Save As option of NotePad or WordPad to save the file with a new file extension .htm.
5. Open the graphical browser.
6. Open the .htm file that you've just saved.
7. If you are successful, you should see your link text underlined.

Here is an example of a discovery journal with the HTML codes added.

Sherry Smith
ONLine Literature
April 4, 1997
<p>
<a href="http://www.interlog.com/~ohi/www/writesource.html">
Writer's Resources on the Web (WWW Virtual Library)</a><p>
Includes links to genres from business writing to travel writing
<p>
<a href="http://the-tech.mit.edu/Shakespeare/works.html">
The Complete Works of William Shakespeare</a><p>

Author: Jeremy Hylton
jeremy@cnri.reston.va.us

PROJECT ASSIGNMENT

Technical reports, clinical findings, and scientific research projects are presented in White Papers. As Web pages, these reports have special HTML
codes for anchors and hypertext links to help users jump from a table of contents to different sections of the report. Open the NotePad or WordPad program and type in the following, substituting the correct information for your
name, college or organization, course name, and date of creation. Copy and
paste your research paper into this coded form where indicated. Save the file
as white.htm

<html><head><title>Your Name White Paper</title></head>
<body bgcolor="ffffff" text="0000ff"link="#ff0000" alink="880088"
vlink="#00ff00">
<a name="back"><font size=5>Student White Paper</font>
<font size=4>Your Name
Research Paper Title</font><p>
<font size=2>Abstract
<blockquote>Write your abstract here. An
abstract is a short, informative description of the contents of the
paper.</blockquote>
<p>
<font size=1>Navigation Bar<p><a href="#paper">Research Paper</a> |
<a href="#works">Works Cited</a> <p>
<hr>
<p>
<blockquote>This is the original work of <a href="mailto: account@
college.edu">Your Name</a>, who has fairly and accurately used information obtained from traditional and electronic sources in a research effort for
Course Name at <a href="http://www.college.edu">College
Name</a>.</blockquote><p>
<font size=1>All rights reserved to this creative work. Date.</font>

<hr size=3>
<a name="paper"> <font size=4>Research Paper</font>
</a>
PASTE YOUR RESEARCH PAPER HERE

```
<p>
<a href="#back">Go Back.</a>
<p>
<a name="works"><center>Works Cited</center></a>
PASTE YOUR WORKS CITED HERE.
<p>
<a href="#back">Go Back.</a>
<p>
```

Explanation
Setting an anchor

1. To mark the place you want to return to (usually at the beginning of the page), put in angle brackets the following code < a name="back">.
2. To set the position within the running page to return to the place called *back* (to make a link), put this code in angle brackets <a href="#back">.
3. When doing the Navigation Bar, set links to the Research Paper and the Works Cited page by putting this code in < a href="#paper">Research Paper</a> and < a href="#works">Works Cited</a>
4. Within the running page, set page anchors in conjunction with titles of the research materials < a name="paper"> and < a name="works">.

Creating hypertext links

1. Within the research paper, identify linkable sources by using a hypertext reference with this code <a href="http://www........">Source name</a>.
2. Load your file white.htm in your browser with File, Open and test your hypertext links.

CHAPTER SEVEN

Search Techniques

Research Agenda

Relevant Resources

Student Paper—Music Therapy

The accumulation of large and sophisticated data bases in the late twentieth century will produce planetary home/commercial high-speed information services utilized by the private user to obtain data for direct personal use.

THE GLOBAL VILLAGE

RESEARCH AGENDA

Technological innovation speeds the research process. Print-based periodical indexes, library card catalogs, and CD-ROM databases are resources common to libraries. However, as the digital revolution of the end of the century expands our access to reference materials available on the World Wide Web, it also complicates the process by which we conduct research, evaluate the findings, and document the material. Traditional forms of research involve settling on a topic, narrowing the topic into a search question, and then locating reference materials related to the subject matter. Transcribing notes from printed material often means hours of copying words from printed sources, followed by more time figuring out how to fit hand-recorded notes into the paper.

The critical thinking involved in deciding on a topic and then formulating a research question remains the same with electronic research methods. Dana Morris, a sophomore honors student, knew immediately that she wanted to research some aspect of music. As a toddler, she loved to sing. Now as a college student, she enjoyed singing in a choir. Thinking about how music helped her to relax, she looked in the library for ways that music changed people's behavior. Finding few sources on her topic, she used a search engine to find Internet sources on music and behavior. Among the sites in her Internet search, she found a credible site sponsored by the American Music Therapy Association, FAQs about Music Therapy (Figure 7.1). This site lead to music therapy programs at the University of Kansas and other links to professional and personal sites. As a result, she narrowed her topic to music therapy and her research question to: How is music therapy used to treat mental patients?

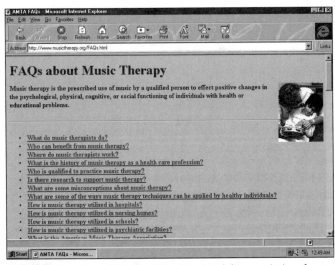

Note: The current URL for this site is different from the URL listed in the student research paper.

FIGURE 7.1 *Music Therapy FAQ. Reprinted, by permission, from the American Music Therapy Association, Inc.*

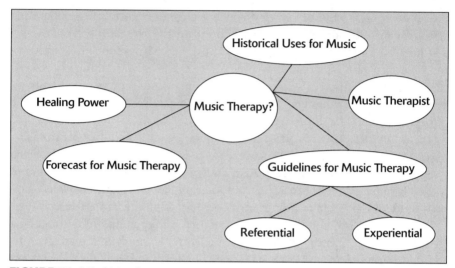

FIGURE 7.2 *Mind Map for Music Therapy*

From a mix of conventional and electronic resources, Dana developed a mind map, similar to the one in Figure 7.2, to help her organize her thoughts from her notes on traditional and electronic resources. She put the narrowed topic at the very heart of the essay.

RELEVANT RESOURCES

Finding Relevant Sites

To continue gathering information, Dana used an array of search engines to find more Internet sources. As she examined these sources, she noted the site's sponsor and assessed the scope of available information. Because she knew about music, she checked the accuracy of statements about music to determine if the site was credible. She also went back to the library to find specific books and articles on music therapy. Dana found that a well-crafted query to a search engine could save many hours of research time.

A **query** is a search statement that contains keywords or complex expressions written as an advanced query. An example of a keyword expression is *music therapy.* When the search requires screening a large amount of potentially unnecessary data, an advanced query uses special operators to show how the keywords are related to one another. These **Boolean operators** are:

and, or, not. Another operator, *near*, may also be used to indicate that a keyword should be found near another keyword. Said another way, a search statement consists of a **character string** formed by keywords with some relationship established by operators in the string.

The following sample statements illustrate a query strategy to gather information about music therapy. Italics denote keywords in the sample expressions, which appear in various combinations suited to the most popular search engine. When query phrasing can use shortcuts with symbols, these shortcuts appear in brackets as an alternate query phrase. Meant to be a general list, some search engines allow for finer distinction than this list suggests.

Query Phrase	Search Results
music [*"music"*]	Finds and publishes all URLs that have *music* in the title or in the content. Using the quotation marks around the phrase can sometimes narrow the list of sites.
mus*	With the wildcard symbol (*), finds and publishes a list with music, muse, musical, etc.
music or therapy [*music	therapy*]	Finds all URLs that have *music,* and then finds and publishes all the URLs that have *therapy*.
music therapy *music* and *therapy* [+music+*therapy*]	Lists Web documents that contain *music* and therapy. Both keywords *music* and *therapy*.
music and not *entertainment* [*music -entertainment*]	Finds all the Web documents that have *music* excluding those documents dealing with *entertainment* before publishing the final list.
music near *therapy*	Publishes a list with sites which have *music* mentioned within 10 words of *therapy*.
music therapy or (*music* and *healing*) [*music therapy* or (+*music+healing*)]	Looks for *music therapy* and then looks again for any documents that contain both keywords *music* and *healing*. The results are published as a list.
(not *entertainment*) and *music*	Finds all Web documents with the keyword *music* and without any mention of *entertainment*.
title: *music* [t:*music*]	Finds and lists all the documents on the WWW with *music* in the title.
url: *music therapy*	Finds and lists all the URLs having information about *music* and *therapy*.

STUDENT PAPER—MUSIC THERAPY

Here is the MLA-style research paper and formal outline that grew out of the mind map in Figure 7.2. Dana Morris combined traditional sources and Web-based sources into a clear and interesting explanation of the background and purposes of music therapy.

Music Therapy
Dana Nicole Morris
English 120 Honors
Dr. Lory Hawkes

September 30, 1996

Outline

History of music

I. Music has been in existence for centuries and aids humans in a variety of tasks.
   A. Findings suggest music existed at least seventy thousand years ago.
   B. Present almost everywhere, music helps us sleep, entertain, and relax.
   C. In addition to the practical uses, music is also used in healing.

Music's potential to soothe and heal the psyche

II. The healing power of music can be looked upon from many different perspectives.
   A. Music is used in conjunction with medicine and results in many advantages in operating rooms.
      1. Diverting patients' attention
      2. Calming the heart
      3. Reducing the use of drugs
   B. Research finds that music influences brain waves and that through combinations of vibrations a patient can be affected both physically and mentally.
   C. The elderly are among those who benefit from music therapy.
      1. Usage in nursing homes
      2. Possible increase in life duration

III. While music has been used for centuries as a therapeutic tool, music therapy was not officially accepted in the medical field until the 1940s.
   A. Music therapy provoked enthusiasm on one side and doubts on the other.
   B. Founded in 1944, the Music Research Foundation's purpose is to advance scientific research into the use of music in relation to medical treatment.

1. Study of recovering veterans
2. Findings about the effects of music

C. The purpose of the National Association for Music Therapy, founded in 1950, is to continue progress in the development of the use of music in therapy.
   1. Definition of music therapy
   2. Registered music therapists

D. William W. Sears and E. Thayer Gaston developed guidelines and principles for music therapy.
   1. Referential music therapy
   2. Experiential music therapy

IV. The music therapist is a professionally trained person who knows how to use music to influence desirable changes in patients.
   A. Many wonder which aspect of music therapy is more important, music skills or therapy skills.
      1. Double-edged sword
      2. Activity vs. therapy
   B. Along with principles and activities, music therapists use specific music therapy techniques.
      1. Guided Imagery and Music (GIM)
      2. Singing and discussion

V. Music therapy allows persons with mental health needs to make positive changes in mood and emotional states and practice problem solving.
   A. Two centuries ago, the physician usually directed treatment, but the music was provided by a musician.
   B. Today, music is administered by a music therapist under an overall treatment plan and is used to specifically meet the needs of patients as prescribed by the doctor.

VI. The future of music therapy is promising.
   A. Documents written by music therapy research teams state the successful results of using music therapy.
   B. Music therapy will continue in success because it is humane and virtually risk-free.

Dana begins her essay with an assessment of the broad appeal of music.

She narrows her focus to a discussion of the importance of music therapy.

Music is everywhere. Some form of music exists in every country and culture. Music is heard in homes, churches, and even workplaces. It helps us sleep, relax, entertain, and concentrate. Unknown by some is the fact that music is also used in healing. Music can treat and heal spiritually, physically, and mentally. Music therapy is a phenomenon that has been practiced for centuries but was not considered an accepted treatment in the medical field until about half a century ago. Music therapy is a significant way to help patients, especially those with mental health needs.

Music has probably been in existence since the beginning of mankind. Cave paintings have been found that strengthen the implication that musical instruments, such as stringed bows, may have been in existence seventy thousand years ago. Also, archeologists have found actual instruments that date back five thousand years (Strauss 48). Not only is music presently practiced worldwide, but it is also an ancient tradition.

Music seems to have never been *only* music. For centuries cultures have used music in various forms of healing. Priests used chants to heal in ancient Greece, India, China, and Egypt. In the European medieval period, in order to analyze pulse rhythms, physicians were required to study music (Gardner 92). Native Americans applied specific songs to different illnesses. The Greeks used music to treat insomnia, anxiety, and poor digestion (Strauss 48). Many other cultures have been using music in healing for hundreds of years.

Music, used in conjunction with medicine, can be considered a medicine in itself. The *National Medical Journal* reported that music diverts the attention of patients while under anesthesia and that music can also calm the heart. Music has had better results than some drugs in treating a lagging bloodstream. The lame have been taught to walk and maniacs have been calmed with the use of music (Langdon 47). Music has been used as a painkiller, and has resulted in terminally ill cancer patients being taken off analgesic drugs and reduced the use of them for mothers in labor (Strauss 51).

Music has an impact on the way people feel. Alvin O. Langdon, author of *Psychosomatic Music*, explains in scientific terms how music can not only affect feelings but also actions. "Research has developed that brain waves have rhythmic patterns, and that music, or tonal vibrations, influence these waves to such an extent that the influence is both physical and mental." The thalamus, the part of the brain that controls sensations, aesthetic feeling, or emotions, is first to pick up tonal vibrations. The cortex, which controls thought and reason, is then stimulated. These powerful vibrations create mental pictures that can affect thought and reason.

The vibrations, produced by force and energy, influence the pictures which can influence action. Langdon believes music is a healer because of the way it affects the brain and

---

Here she develops the chronology of music dating back to cave societies.

She underscores the cultural relevance of music.

Using traditional, print-based sources, Dana carefully constructs the background information needed to understand the importance of music to society, and now she shifts to the newer use of music as a therapy to help people feel better.

that through combinations of tonal vibrations it is possible to control the minds of individuals and point them in a desired direction (47). Studies have linked music to feelings of rest, joy, playfulness, sadness, love, and yearning. Emotionally disturbed patients became calmer, more open, sociable, and helpful to other patients during and after music listening sessions (Strauss 52).

Music is also used in the treatment of Alzheimer's patients. Kay Gardner, composer, teacher, and recording artist shared:

She examines a specific case. The anecdote adds an emotional impact to the essay.

> At the nursing home where I went from room to room entertaining residents with my flute, there was a woman in her eighties suffering from Alzheimer's Disease. Her name was Sophie, and she wandered the halls slowly, supporting herself with two canes. Her eyes had a glazed, uncomprehending look. But as soon as she heard the jaunty flute tunes I played as I walked down the hall, she lifted both her canes, became bright-eyed, and danced a little jig. When the music stopped, Sophie resumed her stooped shuffle with the canes, and the sparkle in her eyes left. (92)

Music has also been related to long life. Dr. John Diamond, author of *Your Body Doesn't Lie*, explains that people's bodies separate good sounds that aid in healing from bad sounds that can be harmful. In his book he included a list of more than one hundred orchestra conductors from age seventy to ninety-six. All presently enjoyed active and healthy lives. In *Inner Rhythm*, Strauss asks, "Why do these busy, productive people defy the life-span statistics of the remainder of the population?" (52).

Using division and classification methods, she names the two poles of music therapy.

She integrates information from a comprehensive FAQ as evidence.

The introduction of music therapy led to two extremes. The first was the enthusiasm that raised blind faith. The other consisted of doubts that prompted ignorant disbeliefs. Juliette Alvin, author of *Music Therapy*, believes that the true essence of music therapy can be defined between the two extremes. She describes music therapy as "a rational discipline which adds to music a new dimension, binding together art, science, and compassion" (3). In "FAQs about Music Therapy," music therapy is defined as "the prescribed use of music by a qualified person to effect positive changes in the psychological, physical, cognitive, or social functioning of individuals with health or education problems" (1).

Music therapy was considered a general treatment—sleep agent or "morale builder"—until after World War II. Music began to be applied more specifically after the war because there was an urge to help hospitalized veterans. Volunteers, including music teachers and school band and choral directors, provided much of the music (Gaston 1). The Music Research Foundation's main objective is to further the research on the use of music as a medical treatment. The foundation, founded in 1944, conducted a study of music as an additional treatment of recovery veterans. The physicians and psychiatrists on the Research Committee reported the following findings:

Here are medical findings to reinforce the claim that music therapy is a viable treatment method.

- Changes in music intensity, rhythm, and dissonant chords produce changes in pulse and respiration.
- Blood pressure rates are affected by music.
- The emotions caused by listening to music can affect the blood supply and change the respiratory rate.
- Various rhythms may improve the listener's eyesight by as much as 25%!
- Music can increase or lessen muscular activity.
- Music increases metabolism and affects digestive, circulatory, and nutritive action. (Strauss 51)

After realizing the significant progress patients made—both physical and emotional—as a result of the many amateur and professional musicians playing for the veterans, doctors and nurses requested that the hospitals hire musicians ("FAQs").

The need for formal training of music therapists became pertinent for evaluation of practice and achievement purposes. In 1944, an institution now known as Michigan State University established the first curriculum to train music therapists. The University of Kansas taught the first course for music therapy in 1946 (Gaston 2).

The National Association for Music Therapy (NAMT) defines music therapy as:

Citing information found at its site, she uses the National Association for Music Therapy as an authoritative source.

the use of music in the accomplishment of therapeutic aims: The restoration, maintenance, and improvement of mental and physical health. It is the systematic application of music, as directed by the music therapist in a therapeutic environment, to bring about desirable changes in behavior. Such changes enable the individual undergoing therapy to experience a greater understanding of himself and the world around him, thereby achieving a more appropriate adjustment of society ("Definitions").

In order to reinforce the credibility of NAMT, she clarifies their purpose.

NAMT, founded in 1950, focuses on the growing use and development of music therapy. NAMT set the standards for training registered music therapists (RMTs) and has promoted research on the benefits of music therapy (FAQs). Individuals may become RMTs after successfully completing extensive training through NAMT's registration program. The Certification Board for Music Therapists (CBMT), independent of NAMT, certifies music therapists through administering an examination that evaluates the individual's knowledge of music therapy and ability to engage in its practices. NAMT is also a member of coalitions which include the Consortium for Citizens with Disabilities, the National Alliance of Pupil Services Organization, and the National Rehabilitation Caucus ("National").

E. Thayer Gaston, editor of *Music in Therapy*, and William W. Sears, a contributor to the book, both of whom are registered music therapists, developed two principal forms of music therapy—referential and experiential, respectively. Dr. Gaston stressed the establishment of interpersonal relationships through music and the development of self-esteem through self-actualization. Dr. Sears stressed self-organization and relations to others in groups (Choi). Together Gaston and Sears developed the following guidelines and principles of music therapy:

- Successful experiences with music lead to feelings of accomplishment and gratification which contribute to self-concept.
- Music is a source of gratification. Music provides opportunities for achievement in noncompetitive situations.
- Music is an emotional expression. Man uses music to express his emotions that are sometimes difficult to express through language.
- Music is structured and time ordered and its predictability provides a basis for anxiety control, cooperation, and purposeful engagement.
- Music triggers memory. Music associates with one's past experience instantly.
- Group participation that is facilitated easily with music leads to feeling needed by others and provides

opportunities for peer approval and acceptance, as well as negative peer sanction for inappropriate behaviors (General).

Byung-Chuel Choi describes a music therapist as a person trained to use music to make desirable changes in patients' conditions with the symbolic use of a double-edged sword. The first side of the sword is the power of music and its esthetic value and the second is its functional role in society. Choi observes that the skillful therapist will use both sides, either switching from one to another as needed or using both at a time. Many wonder which aspect of music therapy is more important, musical skills or therapy skills. Choi reflects:

> I saw some music therapists excited about their activities. They talk about what they did and how well it went. Most of them get proud of having good group leading skills, but frequently miss telling how the patients responded to it. I truly believe that effective therapy lies on the patient's side. It is not an activity to make therapy effective. It is the strategy [concerning] how one operates concepts and principles for the patients' benefit. No matter how wonderful the activity is, if it does not apply to the patient's problem area, it is not therapy. It becomes purely "an activity." What we are doing for patients is "therapy."

In addition to the principles of music therapy and the activities music therapists use, there are also specific music therapy techniques. One method is called Guided Imagery and Music (GIM). GIM is a technique in which classical music is used with relaxation of mind and body to promote self-actualization. The method produces imagery which gives the patient insights of the self that can be used with the help of the therapist. In conjunction with GIM is the "belief that everyone can understand his or her problems and has the ability to overcome the problem within the self." It is for this reason that GIM focuses more on inner awareness than treating symptoms.

Another is the singing and discussion method. The music helps the patients respond to the words of the songs and prompts the patients to share thoughts and feelings associated with the song. First in using this technique the therapist sings songs that are familiar to the patients. Afterwards there is a discussion about the meanings of the songs. The therapist then improvises a song using the words from the shared thoughts of the patients. "This can be a very positive conclusion of the session so that each client might carry over his or her feelings and emotions in productive ways" (Music).

In the eighteenth century, musicians provided the music, and many times patients played music as well, while physicians directed the treatment. Such was the case of a London medical man by the name of Richard Brocklesby, who wrote a treatise on music therapy. Brocklesby's patient lost his two sons in the battle of Dunblain. Brocklesby had his patient listen to music in order to motivate him to play. "In spite of all care taken of him he fell into a nervous fever which left him in so deep a melancholy that he refused the necessary support of food and all discourse with the persons usually conversant about him" (Alvin 46). Brocklesby knew his patient had previously enjoyed playing the harp. After numerous remedies were tried, Brocklesby asked one of the patient's friends to approach him playing soft and solemn music and place his most capable hand on the instrument. The patient did not refuse the transition; in fact, after one or two songs had been played, he rediscovered emotions of mind and body. Brocklesby allowed his patient to play a while everyday until he was encouraged to speak. Shortly afterwards, he began to accept food and medicine which were vital to his condition until finally he completely recovered and returned to his previous state of health (46).

"Music therapy allows persons with mental health needs to: explore personal feelings, make positive changes in mood and emotional states, have a sense of control over life through successful experiences, practice problem solving, and resolve conflicts leading to stronger family and peer relationships" (FAQs). In the hospital, music is administered under an overall treatment designed and prescribed by a physician to specifically fulfill the patient's needs. The music therapist uses music along with his personality and skills to help the patient deal with problems in a better way (Gaston 239). Consider the case of Tex, a twenty-six-year-old man in a wheelchair. His legs were paralyzed, but no test could find a physical reason for his paralysis. In the recreational therapy clinic, Tex talked of his participation in football and basketball, how he had been a cowboy and a rodeo star, and about construction he had done. When he entered the music therapy clinic, he immediately directed his attention to a string bass and replied that he played bull fiddle in Tommy Dorsey's orchestra. When the instrument was placed before him to play, it was obvious he had not played anything like it before. Tex explained that he was "out of shape" and that "no one could play the instrument in a wheelchair." Both the doctor and the music therapist agreed but asked Tex if he would like to play around with it and he accepted. As Tex came to the clinic day after day the staff became certain that he had no prior training in music. No one volunteered to teach him to play; they simply told him he was getting back in shape.

There was a dance combo which included three saxophones, a piano, guitar, drums, and a trumpet which the music therapist played. Tex started to come early to listen to the combo and subtly play along. Many days had passed when the music therapist mentioned that the combo had an open position, and that if Tex could only stand and play he could fill the space. Tex mentioned crutches; they were provided and he was then part of the combo. Although Tex had good rhythm, it was still obvious he could not read music; the staff did not feel it was smart to confront him about his Tommy Dorsey story.

One day Tex heard the chief music therapist say that he was going to a violin lesson. Tex knew that the therapist was a remarkable player and wondered why he was taking lessons. The therapist replied, "You and I know that each of us needs to go back occasionally and refresh himself on the basic fundamentals of his instrument." The next day Tex asked for lessons. Soon he was able to discontinue use of his crutches.

The bass drum player for the hospital concert band left and Tex took his place. One day between numbers, Tex yelled and fainted. When he came to, he was the center of attention. He fainted the next day also and the therapist noticed that Tex fell in a cushioned chair. After the rehearsal the therapist suggested that Tex see his doctor and said, "We will be playing for quite a few things before an audience in the near future, and we just can't take the chance of having a concert disrupted by a fainting spell." Tex fainted no more. Eventually, Tex was discharged and able to readjust to society.

He had learned to satisfy his tremendous need for attention by earning it rather than using his former devices— paralysis, fainting, and grandiose fabrications about his past accomplishments. Many people in the hospital had a part in his treatment, but among the most effective were his doctor, who first detected his interest in music, and the music therapists, who *accepted Tex at his level of functioning*, and helped him supplant his inappropriate attention-getting devices with behavior patterns that *earned* the gratification he needed. (Gaston 246)

Music therapy is the use of music by a trained individual who applies his or her music *and* therapy skills to make positive changes in a patient's condition, be it physical, emotional, or mental. Music therapy has a bright future according to the documents written by music therapy research teams stating the successful results of using music therapy (FAQs). More importantly, music therapy, regardless of its research support, will continue to prosper because it is one of the most humane and risk-free treatments in existence. Who can argue with using something as gentle as music to help someone like Tex? Music does simple things like helping us sleep or relax as well as remarkable things like energizing an Alzheimer's patient and bringing a grieving man out of depression. Music therapy proves to be an effective way to treat a variety of patients.

Works Cited

Alvin, Juliette. *Music Therapy.* New York: Basic, 1975.

Choi, Byung-Chuel. "My Philosophy of Music Therapy." 5 Sep. 1996
    <http://falcon.cc.ukans.edu/~memt/philosophy.html>.

"Definitions of Music Therapy." 13 Aug. 1996
    <http://falcon.cc.ukans.edu/~memt/principles.html>.

"FAQs about Music Therapy." 2 Apr. 1996. 29 Jul. 1996
    <http://www.cais.net.namt/FAQs.html>.

Gardner, Kay. "Music for Relaxation." *The Big Book of Relaxation: Simple Techniques to Control the Excess Stress in Your Life.* Ed. Larry Blumenfeld. Roslyn, NY: Relaxation, 1994.

Gaston, E. Thayer, ed. *Music in Therapy.* New York: MacMillan, 1968.

"General Guidelines and Principles of Music Therapy." 13 Aug. 1996
    <http://falcon.cc.ukans.edu/~memt/principles.html>.

Langdon, Alvin O. *Psychosomatic Music: Tonal Vibrations and their Affect on the Mind of Mankind.* Huntington, WV: Chapman, 1960.

"Music Therapy Method." 5 Sep. 1996
   <http://falcon.cc.ukans.edu/~memt/schools.html>.
"National Association for Music Therapy." 29 Mar. 1996. 21
   Aug. 1996
   <http://www.cais.net/namt/NAMT.html>.
Strauss, Sally. *Inner Rhythm: An Exciting New Approach to
   Stress-Free Living.* San Francisco: Chase, 1984.

Through the Looking Glass

*The following exercises allow you to explore and draw
conclusions about what you see; in essence, you get to be
the expert.*

WEB LINGO

Boolean operators
character string
query

WEB ITINERARY

1. Here is a twist on game shows that present word puzzles to contestants
   to see if they can guess the question. Decide the person, place, or event
   that correctly answers each word puzzle. Write a search statement to find
   a list of Web sites providing more information on each item.

   An unprincipled computer expert
   A place where spacemen are rumored to be detained by the U.S. gov-
   ernment
   An unsinkable English vessel
   An athletic contest dating back to ancient Greece in which the world
   participates every four years
   A time of artistic and cultural achievement in Europe after the Hun-
   dred Years' War

She bears the name of a genre of religious paintings depicting the mother of Christ

A preacher whose dream gave vision to the Civil Rights movement

An "English Rose" whose charitable works are remembered by her subjects

2. Divide into smaller groups and develop brainstorming lists for class research topics. Use e-mail to compile your list of topics and then send the list of research topics to all the members of your class.

3. Separate into small groups for exploring the Web. Brainstorm controversial topics. Find an example of a Web site that gives a balanced discussion of the controversial topic; find an example of a biased Web site about the controversial topic. Report back to the class about how you were able to distinguish between the intent of the sites based on what was said (the content), how it was said (tone), and why it was said (purpose).

4. Search the Web for travel information about a place you would like to visit. How do these travel sites attract users and keep their interest? What kind of information did they give about their services; what kind of information did they withhold?

5. Use a search engine to gather a list of sites about the popular *Star Trek* TV series and movies. Compare the sites in relation to useful content and accurate detail. Are there characteristics that all of the sites have in common? Which site seems to be the best? Why?

PROJECT ASSIGNMENT

The following questions target issues related to the use of the Web. Select one of the research questions, extend the question with a mind map, and compile a discovery journal based on the subject matter. Create a white paper (introduced in the previous chapter) with a link to a Works Cited page. Within the text of the white paper, include hypertext links to Internet sources. This assignment may be done individually or in groups.

• Should the federal government regulate the contents of Web pages to prevent the publication of harmful information like the chemical formula for bombs, such as the one responsible for the Oklahoma City bombing?

• With the growth, popularity, and prosperity of the Web, are we excluding segments of the population from the vast knowledge contained in the Web?

- Do copyright laws need to be revised to protect those who publish on the Web?
- What should the Web community do to protect children who use the Net from pornography?
- What is the technological imperative?
- When is electronic commerce a risk to free enterprise?
- Who are the heroes of the digital revolution?

CHAPTER 8
Basic Authoring

Mapping the Landscape

Hypertext Markup Language

> *As you may be sure that the emerging mediums . . . will intensify the attack on the printed word as the "sole" container of the public mentality, without being aware of it, of course. By the twenty-first century, most printed matter will have been transferred to something like an ideographic microfiche as only part of a number of data sources available in acoustic and visual modes.*
>
> THE GLOBAL VILLAGE

MAPPING THE LANDSCAPE

To be a Web page developer, an author must be able to landscape a Web page with text, pictures, hypertext links, and graphical elements much like an artist combines shapes, colors and textures on a canvas. If a Web page starts a series of pages, it is a home page. Figure 8.1 shows a common layout for a home page, which should have these characteristics:

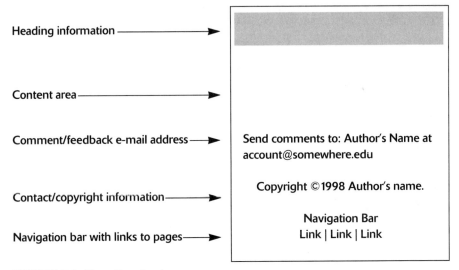

FIGURE 8.1 *Home Page Landscape*

- Sets out the theme in the heading information
- Gives an overview in the content area
- Identifies the owner/author/Web administrator
- Clarifies restrictions on the use of the content
- Establishes a year or date for the page's creation or update (may contain a counter)
- Provides quick orientation to the site's purpose
- Supplies a means link to subsequent pages or other Web sites

If a home page is successful, it imparts its theme and its tone in a powerful way. However, the impact of the home page does not come from the technical wizardry, but rather from human expression so complete or so well said that we return over and over again to experience it. Information design does help promote the message. For our purpose of learning how to design information, we will concentrate on three formats (Figure 8.2): a running **list,** a compact **table,** and a segmented page with **frames.**

First, if the format is a running list, information flows continuously down a page with headings that signal relationships between text, images, and hypertext links inserted here or there to provide a way to go to another logically related destination. Users travel through the list by reading headings down the page or by skipping to an important area in the text with page anchors, which are invisible bookmarks.

Second, if the format is a compact table, an array of columns and rows organize information to fit the viewing window of the browser. Finally, if the

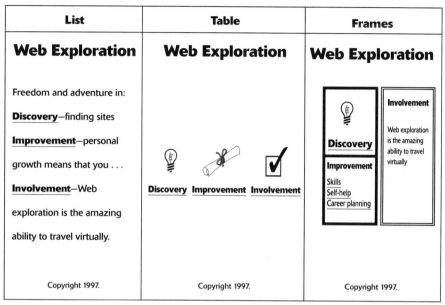

FIGURE 8.2 *Three Formats for Web Pages*

format is frames, segments of text or images appear as separate windows with scrollbars or movable borders. Frames accentuate comparisons between the windows and may reduce the need for separate pages of explanations. The most compact form of Web page design, frames have one drawback—not all browsers can display or copy them. Often Web pages offer a frames version of the Web page as well as a plain text version.

To understand the appeal of a home page, you need to understand design principles that contribute to its sense of credibility, emotional appeal, and logical order. Whether the format is simple or complex, a good home page draws users in and makes them want to explore it. Shortlist 26 highlights the Yale Style Manual that offers additional discussion on Web page design.

SHORTLIST 26
Web Page Style Manual

Yale Style Manual
http://info.med.yale.edu/caim/stylemanual/Manual_Intro.HTML

Home Page Design

If a home page is an exercise in language and art to describe, explain, or argue a topic, then its visual and verbal language ought to be effective and in keeping with the purpose of the site. There are three ways to accomplish effective communication of ideas: authority, emotion, and logic.

Authority.   A home page is worth the time to explore it if it clearly, accurately, and sufficiently expresses the development of ideas and links related to the purpose of the site. A case in point is the Library of Congress home page. It is always accurate and attractive. Written for the general public, the nontechnical descriptions, thorough samplings of art or historical events, and flawless execution of links to other sites, build and satisfy high expectations. Not only is this home page frequently revised, it continually links to expansions of its features. As part of the Web community, the Library of Congress is a valuable public service site for its authenticity.

Another useful site is the *Chronicle of Higher Education* (Figure 8.3). This time-honored publication has its name centered in the heading information area, followed by the date of the publication. The *Chronicle* lists weekly features in hypertext links of patriotic blue and red against a white background; a large picture related to the print-based feature story completes the home page. Its discussions of issues related to education and society are widely respected for their fairness and timeliness. The site builds good will among

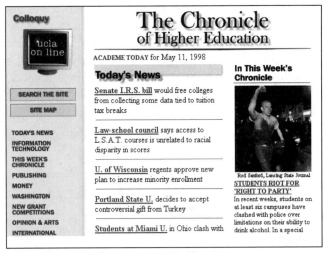

FIGURE 8.3 *Authority. Reprinted, by permission, from the Chronicle of Higher Education.*

frequent users by offering salary surveys, job postings, reviews of innovative projects, and advisories on personal finances for educators.

Emotion.   Emotion can make Web users more receptive to the content, tone, and purpose of a Web site. For example, the Blue Ribbon Campaign home page (Figure 8.4) situates its icon opposite a picture of the Statue of Liberty in the heading information area. At the same time its free speech slogan appeals to our patriotism. In effect, the page appeals to our pride and sense of freedom of choice, and capitalizes on our fear of losing our privacy and limiting our choices because of censorship and regulation. The page also declares it is one of the "most-linked-to-pages on the entire World Wide Web" as proof of the Web community's endorsement of its activities. Further visual evidence of support from the virtual community is displayed by other sites that use the blue ribbon icon to link back to the campaign's home page.

Logic.   The AskERIC home page (Figure 8.5) employs a table format that fills up the screen. The page offers a vertical and horizontal sequence of options

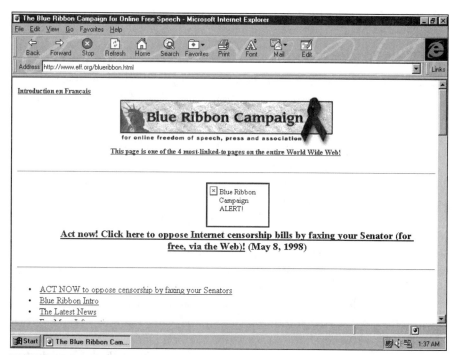

FIGURE 8.4 *Blue Ribbon Campaign. Reprinted, by permission, from the Electronic Freedom Foundation.*

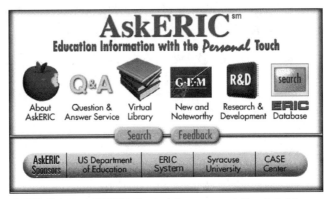

FIGURE 8.5 *AskERIC's Logical Arrangement. Reprinted, by permission, from the ERIC Clearinghouse.*

and supplies a navigation bar to explore the Web. Well designed and thought out, the page has a logical arrangement of hot buttons for quick access and a sequence of text and graphics in rows and columns. Its user-friendly approach, attractive and functional organization, and its wealth of information enable this site to stand on its own merits in persuading visitors about its worth.

Web Page Composition

To design an effective Web page, you translate your ideas into an expression that is logical, clear, and direct. Its organization should anticipate the needs and mistakes of potential users. A Web page is like an expressive essay in which you examine a subject and develop reasons for your point of view.

In the beginning, the writing process for a Web page is similar to the traditional essay. First, there is the time of invention in which an idea comes to you. Enlarging the idea with any prewriting strategies often takes the form of brainstorming or mind-mapping in which you freely list expanded ideas associated with your subject or the form of questioning in which you ask yourself the journalist's questions of who, when, what, why, and how. To record prewriting inspirations, both authors and Web page designers write notes in a list with topics and subtopics, or draw a mind map with thoughts linked to one another in a flow chart. In the drafting stage, however, the writing process changes (Figure 8.6). Although the author of an essay would normally start writing the essay, at this point a Web author searches to survey the kinds of Web pages that already exist on the topic and to assess the competition.

From the standpoint of knowing the competition, Web authors draft a page or pages that relate the subject from their point of view, conduct another

Essay	Web Page
Invention	Invention
Prewriting strategies	Prewriting strategies
Brainstorming	Brainstorming
Questioning	Questioning
Free writing	Free writing
Mind map	Mind map
Drafting and Feedback	Survey competing pages
Revision	Gather images, icons, backgrounds
Publication	Design
To the professor	Initial Web page design
To the class	Feedback
To a community	Revision
	Revision as a local file
	Revision as a public file
	Publication
	Announcement through e-mail
	Announcement to search engines

FIGURE 8.6 *Essay Process versus Web Page Design Process*

search to find hypertext links to allied Web pages, organize and usually annotate the links, and gather more graphics and special elements to individualize their page from other Web pages. Colleges and universities may allot temporary space on the Web server to students to build personal Web pages. The Web administrator or a handbook supplies information about acceptable use policies and Web publishing procedures. Mounting a personal Web page through a local Internet service provider or a commercial Internet service provider may involve sending the page to the provider through a file transfer process or by attaching the Web page as an e-mail. The new browsers include a publishing feature that makes ftp quick and easy.

Web page authors want feedback from their friends, educators, and people they consider to be experts before the page is publicized widely. On the basis of this feedback, the author revises the pages, updates any broken hypertext links to pages that are no longer situated at the referenced URL, and officially publishes the page by adding its URL to the databases of popular search engines.

A Web page is never meant to be static. The page should be in constant revision as its information changes, as link locations to other sites change, as newer, worthy sites appear, and as the author's knowledge and ability to use the hypertext markup language improves. Because the true measure of a

Web page's success is the number of visitors who find and reuse the information, an author needs to remember these essential characteristics:

- Content that is clear and direct, aided by grammatically correct expression
- Graphic elements that are relevant, attractive, fitted to the space
- Links that are logical extensions to the page's discussion and accurately connected
- Special elements like animation, sound, color, texture that are consistent with the page's purpose, content, and landscape

Although style manuals offer common models, personal creativity and verbal expression are important and may be the factors that distinguish the Web page from all others.

HYPERTEXT MARKUP LANGUAGE (HTML)

As a composite of visible information and invisible HTML, the Web page is a document that requires coding to generate its appearance and functional ability. **Hypertext Markup Language (HTML)** is an English-based system of indicating the purpose of each element of a document with the use of angle brackets that form **tags.** As the very first element of any HTML document, the beginning tag identifies the nature of the document.

<html>

Although tags usually appear in pairs on either side of an expression,

Welcome

the beginning html tag must also be the ending tag as the very last expression in an HTML document. As an ending tag, it has a forward slash within the angle brackets like this:

</html>

The new browsers and other software applications offer powerful Web page composers that enable Web developers to create pages without knowing how to use the tags. Two of the leading Web page editors are Microsoft's Front Page and Adobe PageMill. But if you do not understand how the tags work when you use these editors, you may not be able to troubleshoot a problem with the page's design or function. These composers offer a what-you-see-is-what-you-get, or **WYSIWYG**, environment meaning that the page can be designed with the same scale fonts, embedded images, and colorful backgrounds that would appear in the final version. Working from the **source code** means that you understand the functions of the codes as you add them to the content of your page.

No matter if you use a Web page **editor** or you compose the document with source codes, every Web page has two main divisions, the *head* and the *body*. What follows are simple instructions about the codes that can appear in each part. The codes relate to a hypertext resume that has the entire source code at the end of this chapter. A comprehensive list of HTML codes appears on page 179.

Head

The head contains HTML coding (Figure 8.7), invisible to the viewer of a browser displaying a Web page, that sets out the official name of the page, or its title.

Tag	Description
<head></head>	Opens and closes the first major portion of the HTML document.
<title></title>	Specifies the public name of the page so that search engines can categorize it. The title should be a noun phrase that identifies the subject matter of the Web page. Vague titles like General or Miscellaneous or single word, broad categories like Resume or Information are poor titles.

FIGURE 8.7 *Head Codes*

Here is a sample of the tags as they appear in the first portion of a hypertext resume. Authors **nest** tags inside one another, using a closing tag to turn off the innermost expression, and then another tag for the next expression, and so on.

```
<html>
    <head><title>Harvey Brown's Resume</title></head>
```

Body

The second broad division of an HTML document is the body which contains the visible content of the Web page and codes for special effects like background color and images, link information, and special elements. The basic HTML codes are in Figure 8.8.

Tag	Description
<body></body>	Opens and closes the body portion.
<h1></h1>	Specifies the largest/boldest font for a heading. The range of headings are <h1> to <h6>, which is the smallest. These headings are boldfaced and carry extra spacing around them.
 	Break or single space functions like a carriage return on a typewriter to wrap to the next line.
<p>	Paragraph or double space gives a clear line after a heading or between paragraphs.
<dl>	Provides a data list item usually at the left margin and when used with <dd> a data item, indented from the left margin.
<blockquote></blockquote>	Indents from the left and right margin so that the expression between the tags seems to be a block of text.
<spacer=#>	Indents the following text from the margin like a tab.
	Specifies the justification of the expression between the tags. Other tags are <left> and <right>.
<address></address>	Provides a way to give feedback to the author and includes an e-mail address.

FIGURE 8.8 *Body Codes*

Links

Contained within the body of an HTML document are reference points or **pointers** to other Web pages or documents. There are two types of links in our model hypertext resume. The first type is a Netscape-specific code that summons an e-mail composition form addressed to the Web page author. The HTML code is used in conjunction with the <address> tag. In the example below, the visible text is "Send comments to:" and the author's name is a link to an e-mail form. When appearing on the published page, the visible text looks like this:

Send comments to: Susan Lark.

The code looks like this:

```
<address>
   Send comments to: <a href="mailto: slark@clarion.edu">Susan Lark.</a>
</address>
```

The navigation bar contains the second type of link in our model hypertext resume. In essence, the bar is a sequence of links to the author's subsequent pages or to other pages. Descriptive phrases identify the travel options. In large, graphics-laden Web sites, navigation bars provide a plain text alternative for browsers that do not recognize graphics. Often the plain words help new users to find their way around more quickly. The navigation bar is centered above the two choices separated by a pipe or " | " mark. The first link specifies a URL, while the second specifies a **relative URL** which links to a subsequent page in the author's directory of files. The visible text looks like this:

Navigation Bar

Return to Clarity College Home Page | My Favorite Links

The code has a <center> alignment and two links:

```
<center>Navigation Bar<br>
<a href="http://www.clarity.edu" >Return to Clarity College Home Page</a> |
<a href="favorite.htm" >My Favorite Links</a></center>
```

Typography

Early printers in the fifteenth through seventeenth centuries viewed themselves as philosophers and designers. They worked with a medium of wooden blocks to create a series of letters sharing a common style and orientation, which we call a **font**. They passed down their art to their apprentices by writing technical manuals about the printing press and the printing process.

Typography is an art and a competency in selecting the typestyle, font size, color, and orientation to give emphasis to what is said, to give feeling to an expression, or to denote subordination. In effect, font size distinguishes headings, color adds mood and tone, and type orientation contributes to the formality or informality of the document. Web authors may create typography for their pages using graphics imported from a graphics software package. However, attractive typography can be achieved through a simple process of coding (Figure 8.9).

Description	HTML Code	Range of Effects
Headings	<h#> Text</h#>	<h1>Largest/Bold</h1> <h6>Smallest/Bold<h6>
Font Size	<font size=#></font>	<font size=1>Smallest</font> <font size=3>Default size</font> <font size=7>Largest</font>
	<font="arial"></font>	<font="arial"> displays the font style called for, provided that the browser recognizes its style
	<big></big>	Big font size
	<small></small>	Small font size
Font Color	<font color="#ffffff"></font>	white
	<font color="#ff0000"></font>	red
	<font color="#00ff00"></font>	green
	<font color="#0000ff"></font>	blue
	<font color="#000000"></font>	black
Font Orientation	<b></b>	bold
	<em></em>	emphasis (italics)
	<strong></strong>	strong emphasis (bold)
	<i></i>	italics
	<cite></cite>	citation in italics
	<u></u>	underline
		subscript
		superscript
	<tt></tt>	typewriter font
	<pre></pre>	preformatted text
Font Effect (blink)	<blink></blink>	texts blinks on and off
Text Justification	<center>.</center>	centers the expression
	<left> </left>	default setting if none specified
	<right> </right>	aligns expression to the right
	<spacer=#>	tabs over the number of pixels
Special Characters	&copy	copyright ©
	&reg	registered TM ®
	&amp	ampersand &
	&quot	quotation marks "
	&lt	less than symbol <
	&gt	greater than symbol >
Linked Text	<body link="009900">	link (green)
	<body alink="990000">	active link (red)
	<body vlink="330066">	visited link (purple)

FIGURE 8.9 *Font Codes*

Font Color

With early Web pages, any underlined text in a blue color meant a hypertext link. As time went by, authors wanted more freedom to experiment with and change font color. On a Web page, color may be specified by the color name like red, blue, green, etc. Selected hues can be set out with a numerical statement to show the appropriate color mix of red, green, and blue. The number is enclosed in quotation marks, preceded by a number sign and has the first two numbers dedicated to red, the second two numbers to green, and the last two numbers devoted to blue. To understand the structure, you need to realize that the number base is 16. From 0–9 are standard numbers, but 10–16 are represented by letters A–F. To call for the deepest color means using the hex number ff. To illustrate, the expression that would give a bright blue color to the body text would be as follows with the red, green, and blue drivers in this order:

Three other ways to give text a color include identifying the text expression as a hypertext link somewhere else. Normally, a link may transform into different colors to serve as a visual cue that a process is or is about to be completed. Although the choice of link color is arbitrary, link colors can convey a mood. Warm colors range from red, to orange, to yellow. Cool colors range from blue, to green, to purple. Of course, in order to be visible, link colors should contrast with the background color or background image of the Web page. Although the default color of text is black against a grey background with a blue link color, if the preferences in the browser call for a white background, the setting will supercede any code in your document.

Here are the three types of links (Figure 8.10) with the equivalent hex codes for green text (link), red text (active link), and purple text (visited link). To help you select hues that are appropriate for your Web page, a more extensive color chart showing groups of colors to support themes appears on the inside front cover of this book.

An example of how text color and link color is assigned appears in the following example. Notice that the <body> tag has been explanded to include text and link color assignments.

<body text="#0000ff" link="#00ff00" alink="#ff0000" vlink="#330066">

Another way using color names would be:

<body text="blue" link="green" alink="red" vlink="purple">

Type	Explanation	HTML Code
Link	expression is a potential link to another URL	link="#00ff00" [green underlined text]
Active link	expression is currently activated by a mouse click	alink="#ff0000" [red underlined text]
Visited link	expression shows that the link has been explored	vlink="#330066" [purple underlined text]

FIGURE 8.10 *Link Codes*

Color Variance

Not all users will have monitors capable of 256 colors. Some mixed colors may not appear as designed on all browsers. It is best to test a Web page on a variety of monitors and browsers before publicly publishing as a Web page on the Internet. Also, the Web author should keep in mind that colors can be distracting to some users and color combinations popular in the United States may have a different impact on international users. Care should be taken to maintain a consistency of color cues for links and body text throughout a layered document. Because a hex conversion color chart is very helpful to have when designing Web pages, you can refer to the sites in Shortlist 27 or use a search engine to find others.

SHORTLIST 27
Color Charts and Advice

Doug Jacobson's Color Chart
http://www.missouri.edu/~jourmlm/356/triplets.html

Netscape Color Pages
http://www.onr.com/user/lights/netlinks.html

Victor Engel's Netscape Color Palette
http://www.onr.com/user/lights/netcol.htmWeb

Engineers Toolbox
http://www59.metronet.com/colors

Lynda Weinman's Browser Safe Palette
http://www.lynda.com/hex.html

Doug Jacobson's color chart has a graduated color scale with each color associated with a specific hex code number. The Engineers Toolbox contains an image map with rows of colors from which a user can pick a color and have the hex number for that color displayed along with the color. Lynda Weinman's site offers two different organizations of color palettes with the hex code embedded in the color box. Netscape Navigator 4.0 and Internet Explorer 4.0 have editors that enable an author to click on a color grid to test a font color or background color.

Spacing and Indention Elements

To bring attention to ideas or the categories of information, Web authors use spacing attributes to set off text with white space, indent passages, organize an array of lists, and interject horizontal lines.

Spacing	Explanation	HTML Code
Spacing	Line break goes to the very next line like a carriage return	
Double space	Paragraph produces a clear line between text blocks	<p>
Preformatted	Maintains all spacing of inserted text; text becomes a block that does not respond to any other style codes	<pre>
Horizontal space	Gives horizontal white space in and around text and graphics; number specifies pixels	<hspace=99>
Vertical space	Gives vertical white space in and around text and graphics; number specifies pixels	<vspace=99>
Horizontal rule	Horizontal line divides parts of an HTML page Other options increase the width or height of the line: <hr size=7> or <hr=100> or <hr width=25%>	<hr>
Horizontal alignment	Align left (default alignment) Other options are: right, center	<right></right>

FIGURE 8.11 *Spacing Codes*

Spacing	Explanation	HTML Code
From both margins	Blockquote	<blockquote>..</blockquote>
From both margins (italics)	Citation	<cite></cite>
Clear separations	Division	<div></div> or <div align=center></div>
Tab	Spacer	<spacer=#> or <spacer height=# width=#>

FIGURE 8.12 *Indention Codes*

Indented passages which can highlight quoted material or add attractive white space to blocks of text can be achieved with simple codes (Figure 8.12).

Vertical lists arrange information in a sequence. They have bullets or numbers preceding the list items, or they can simply have one line starting at the leftmost margin with a subordinate item indented beneath. The HTML codes (Figure 8.13) specify which kind of spacing the items will have. The resume at the end of this chapter uses an unordered list <ul> in conjunction with bulleted list items <li>.

List	Explanation	HTML Code
Definition list	Interweaves term and definition [Used with <dt> term and <dd> definition]	<dl></dl>
Directory	List of items each less than 20 characters	<dir></dir>
Menu	Interactive list	<menu></menu>
Ordered list	Indented consecutively numbered list items	<ol></ol>
Unordered list	Indented bulleted list items	<ul></ul>

FIGURE 8.13 *List Codes*

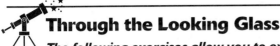

Through the Looking Glass

The following exercises allow you to explore and draw conclusions about what you see; in essence, you get to be the expert.

WEB LINGO

editor

font

frames

Hypertext Markup
  Language (HTML)

list

nest

pointers

relative URL

source code

table

tags

WYSIWYG

WEB ITINERARY

1. Consider how the writing style, tone, and amount of detail changes from a newspaper medium to a Web page. Clip an important news story from the newspaper. After dividing the story into topical areas, create a Web page using the following topic model with large headings to distinguish the topical areas. Explore the Web and find other resources for each topical area. Within the content, make hypertext links to other Web resources. End with sources using the proper form of citation to give credit to your print-based and Internet-based sources and acknowledgments for special help on the project.

2. Design a simple Web page that tells about the freshman experience at your college. Ask for feedback from the counselors at your college/ university.

3. Use a search engine to find more HTML style guides. Prepare a discovery journal that gives a brief description of each style guide. Compose a Web page that gives your information to your class with links to those style guides.

TOPIC

Institution

Authors

Purpose of the project.

Subtopic 1

Write an explanation here making sure that you use hypertext links to Web resources. To make a phrase in text a hypertext link to its Web URL use the following HTML code: <a href="http://...">Name of Web Resource</a>

Subtopic 2

Write an explanation here making sure that you use hypertext links to Web resources.

Sources

Use the proper forms of citation to list the print-based or Web-based sources.

Put contact and copyright information last.

4. In small groups of three or four members, collect the favorite joke of each member. Compose a list format home page for all of the jokes. Begin with a list of the categories of jokes and use a descriptive name to indicate the theme of each joke within the category.

PROJECT ASSIGNMENT

A resume is a positive assessment of your potential and accomplishments. As such, it takes on a traditional, print-based organization with a few changes in personal information to protect you in the digital age. For instance, your address is your e-mail address, not your street address and home phone number. HTML tags ensure vertical and horizontal spacing, font emphasis, and attractive overall design. Type this code in substituting your individual information. When you graduate you may need a print-based resume, a plain text resume that can be e-mailed, and a Web page resume like the one below.

```
<html><head><title>Your Name's Resume</title></head>
<body bgcolor="#ffffff" text="#0000ff" link="#ff0000" vlink="#000000"
alink="#0f0ff0">
<center><h2>Your Name</h2></center>
<p>
<ul>
<li><b>Qualifications</b><p>
    <ul>
    <li>Most important qualification
    <li>Second most important
      qualification
    <li>Third most important
      qualification

    </ul>
<p>
<li><b>Education</b><p>
<blockquote>College Name<br>
Your Major<br>
Graduation Date: 99/99/99, GPA: 9.9</blockquote>
<p>
<blockquote>Previous College, Location<br>

Program/major<br>
Degree or Accumulated Hours</blockquote>
<p>
<ul>
<li><b>Experience</b><p>
<blockquote>Company Name, Location [from—to dates]<br>
Your Job Title: Description of duties</blockquote>
<p>
<blockquote>Company Name, Location [from—to dates]<br>
Title: Description of duties</blockquote>
<p>
</ul>
<hr size=2>
<address>
```

> **Writing Tips**
>
> Employers learn who you are from your emphasis on what you think is important. Dates should be accurate and job titles should be explained with a description of your duties, especially any training or supervision of other employees. A list of references should not be given. If you are a student with many years of work experience, go back to the last five years in that category. This is a list format Web page.

Send comments to: <a href="ailto: account@college.edu">Your name</a>
</address>
<p>
<center>Copyright 1997. All rights reserved.
The individual named on this page has prepared all the information and ver-
ifies its authenticity.<p>
<a href="URL">Return to Your Home Page</a>
</body>
</html>

CHAPTER 9
Advanced Authoring

| Icons and Images
| Special Elements
| Storyboarding

> *This new interplay between word and image can be understood if we realize that our skulls really contain two brains straining to be psychically united.*
>
> THE GLOBAL VILLAGE

ICONS AND IMAGES

Icons

An icon is a common visual symbol that represents something. An icon can be used on a Web page to indicate a purpose, a place, a thing, or a special function. For example, both Netscape and Internet Explorer have a button called Back that provides a means to redisplay the previously viewed Web page. The arrow is an icon, or a visual substitute for the function "to return."

Images

An image can be a digitized masterpiece like the Mona Lisa, a brightly colored photograph, a three-dimensional view of a room, or even a line drawing of a cartoon figure. Two of the most popular formats for images used on Web pages are **Graphics Interchange Format (gif)** or a **Joint Photographic Experts Group (jpeg** or **jpg)**. Although there is some debate about which format is better, experts believe that simple images should be gifs and more complex images like photographs should be jpegs. Of course, images require more memory space to store, and they can also add more time to the loading process of a Web page which contains them. Some Web users disable their browser's ability to display images—in order to speed up the loading of Web pages in a text-only format. A few text-only browsers still exist, but over 90 percent of today's browsers are graphical, capable of displaying text and graphics.

Just like software, images may be easy to acquire on the Web, but they may not be free to use. If the site or Web author provides a written release to freely use the image, then the image is free. However, if the author or site puts limitations on the way the image can be reused, the image remains copyrighted and restricted from general use. Some sites like NASA offer a library of freely downloadable images; other sites like Kodak expressly forbid the commercial reuse of their photographs but permit the private, educational use of the site's photographs.

Web authors can create their own images with a graphics software package like Adobe Photoshop or Corel Draw or simple graphics programs like PC Paint. In addition, software programs like LviewPro or PaintShop Pro enable Web authors to capture an image from a Web site, change the file format of an image, edit the image, and reduce its size to a **thumbnail** image, which is a smaller (20–70 kilobyte) representation of the image at its source URL. The thumbnail may be a link to a larger version of the work stored at a different URL. The thumbnail image (usually 100 pixels wide and 100 pixels high) gives a sense of what the link will show, but significantly decreases the loading time of the Web (Figure 9.1).

Occasionally, Web authors embed a program code that defaces an image or superimposes the company's logo as a **watermark**, thereby showing the source of the file, or a program code that disables the download function. Computer viruses can also disrupt the capture of graphic files.

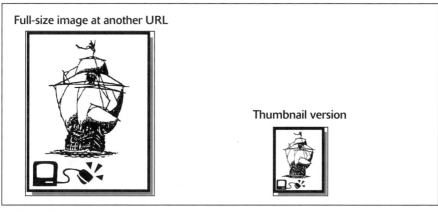

FIGURE 9.1 *Image Size*

Images may be downloaded from ftp sites, gopher sites, or sent as attachments to e-mail. To save **bandwidth** and therefore time during the electronic transfer of the image from one computer to another, images, text files, and program files may be compressed and decompressed with a popular shareware program like WinZip or Pkzip (Figure 9.2) that reads a variety of compression schemes. To understand which compression scheme is active, the program examines the three-character extension to the filename (Figure 9.3). To use the file, you must have a program that interprets the compression scheme.

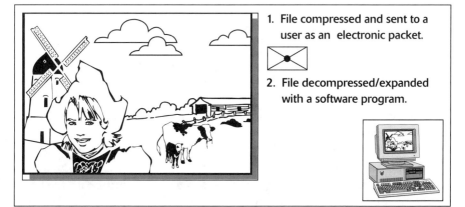

FIGURE 9.2 *Image Compression Process*

Scheme	File Extension	Description
text	.doc	Plain text file (ASCII) that may be usable as is; easily imported into Windows 95 WordPad and Microsoft Word
	.txt	Plain text file (ASCII) that may be usable as is; easily imported into Windows 95 WordPad and most word processors
	.ps	PostScript file that may be usable as is with an Adobe PostScript text reader or a PostScript printer
binary	.LZH	DOS file that decompresses with WinZip
	.zoo	DOS or UNIX file decompresses with a ZOO program
	.zip	A UNIX file that decompresses with an unZIP program
	.shar	A UNIX file that decompresses with a SHAR program
	.tar	A UNIX file that decompresses with a TAR program

FIGURE 9.3 *Sample Compression Schemes*

GIF Images.   Initially created by CompuServe for its commercial Internet service, gifs are compatible with most graphical browsers. Gifs may be part of larger, more complex drawings called **image maps** that contain rectangular or circular hot spots which hold links to other URLs. An example of an image map appears in Figure 9.4. In the figure, each balloon labeled with a subject is actually a hypertext link to a URL. When the user clicks within the circular area of a colored balloon, the browser goes to the predefined URL and displays what is there. Two shareware programs, MapThis! and MapEdit, offer an easy way to make image maps. Shortlist 28 contains other graphics software available for free downloading.

Two important types of gif images are a regular gif, sometimes known as an *87a*, and an extended gif, known as an *89a*. The latter gif can be created as a **transparent** image because the image's background merges with the background color or texture of the page. In the example of Figure 9.4, the background behind the balloons is the same color as the background of the Web page. Transparent gifs produce sharper, less cluttered Web pages. Another

---

SHORTLIST 28
Image Manipulation Software

LviewPro
http://www.lview.com/

PaintShop Pro
http://www.computeng.com.au/

MapEdit
http://www.boutell.com/mapedit/

MapThis!
http://www.incontext.ca/demo/mapthis.html

WinZip
http://www.winzip.com/

Pkunzip
ftp://ftp.pkware.com/pub/pkware/pkz204g.exe

---

form of the 89a gif is the **animated** gif. Saved as a multilayered image, the animated gif repositions figures in an image ever so slightly so that each layer produces a small range of movement. A well-constructed image moves. The dragon in the hot air balloon on the Netscape advisory page is an 89a gif, as is the American flag blowing in the wind on the White House Web page.

A gif image, referred to as a bit-mapped image, may be a gradient of grey, called **grayscale**, or it can possess 2, 4, 8, 16, 32, 64, 128 or even a maximum of

FIGURE 9.4 *Image Map*

256 colors, even though there may be a potential for over 16 million colors. The number of colors and the actual dimensions of the gif affect the loading time and memory storage requirements of an image. For instance, a 16-color gif, saved as a thumbnail, will load more quickly than a 256-color gif. If the color scheme of the image is simple, there is no need to use more colors.

Another thing affecting memory size and loading time of a gif image is the process of correcting the color through **dithering.** In this process, the color scheme may be changed or distorted as colors are adjusted by a graphics software program. To address the slow-to-reveal image problem, Web authors employ a technique called **interlacing**. With a graphics software program, the image is saved in a gif format so that it appears gradually, rather than waiting until the entire graphic loads to reveal any portion of the gif image. Numerous sites make gif images available for downloading. Some sites also include creative images for bullets and horizontal rules. Shortlist 29 provides Web sites offering a variety of images, even animated gifs.

JPEG Images.   At the other end of the image spectrum is the jpeg file. Unlike gifs, jpegs are ideal to display a complex image like a photograph or a digitized work of art because they offer a small memory size to speed the electronic transfer from the Web source to a user's browser with a minimum of color loss and a maximum of contrast. As a rule, jpegs save as small images

---

SHORTLIST 29
Image Sources

Web Developer's Virtual Library
http://WWW.Stars.com/Authoring/Graphics

Animated GIF Artists Guild (AGAG)
http://www.agag.com/makeown.html

Dutchman's Library of Animated GIFs
http://www.vuurwerk.nl/levon/animated.html

Animated Gifs from Netscape
http://home.netscape.com/assist/net_sites/starter/samples/animate.html

TRU Reality
http://www.webgrafx-fx.com

WWW Icons and Logos
http://www-ns.rutgers.edu/doc-images/

and the browser increases them in size when it loads them. As a result, the starting image's crispness is conveyed to the larger version. Unlike gifs, jpegs do not need to be dithered, and they cannot be transparent. However, a new process called a progressive jpeg shows a vaguely defined image which gradually sharpens to its full contrast.

Inline Images.   Images should be integrated into a page. When they are embedded in the source code of a Web page, they are called **inline images.** Inline images can come from a file on a floppy drive or hard drive, a URL, or refer to a partial URL. The image source tag defines the location of the image and gives additional information about how to situate the image on the page. Naturally, in order to call in an image from a URL, the graphical browser should be connected to the Internet by a **live connection.** Depending on the image's location, the image source tag <img src> for the file book.gif can have different path statements as URLs (Figure 9.5).

Unlike MS-DOS commands which require the user to specify a source drive along with a drive letter and a filename like c:/author/book.gif, the

Location	Explanation	HTML Code
floppy drive	To test the display, Web developers often put all the files on a floppy to test links and appearance. Because the floppy drive is already established as the source drive, only the filename is needed.	<img scr="book.gif">
hard drive	A subdirectory of a hard drive with the computer already pointing to the hard drive	<img src="author/book.gif">
full URL	From a Web site	<img src="http://www.xnow.com/pix/book.gif">
partial URL	From a Web site that is already selected through the browser	<img src="newday/graphics/book.gif">

FIGURE 9.5 *Image Path Statement Codes*

HTML commands determine whether the browser is already pointing to the source drive or a Web location. In many cases, it may be quicker to reference the URL within the image tag as the source so that when the page is loaded, the browser will go out and find the URL and load its contents. If this is the case, less space will be needed on the server to store the Web pages.

Images can be adjusted in height, width, and alignment in relation to the text. They can also have a border, no border, or be surrounded by white space. If the image has a border but is also a link somewhere else, its border color will be the same color specified as the link color.

The following HTML sample shows codes to display an inline image on a local file which starts at the left margin and has a 4-pixel border.

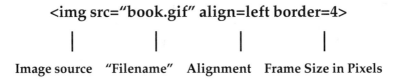

<img src="book.gif" align=left border=4>

Image source   "Filename"   Alignment   Frame Size in Pixels

The remaining examples show how alignment affects an image with no border. If no alignment is specified, a default alignment positions the image at the left margin with the text starting at the bottom of the image. Figure 9.6 shows how alignment affects text placement. In addition to placing an image at the left, center, or right and aligning it at the top, middle, or bottom, a Web

Appearance	Explanation	HTML Code
Text starts here.	Top alignment	<img src="book.gif" align=top border=0>
Text starts here.	Middle alignment.	<img src="book.gif" align=top border=0>
Text starts here.	Bottom alignment.	<img src="book.gif" align=top border=0>

FIGURE 9.6 *Image Alignment Codes*

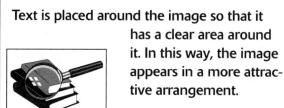

FIGURE 9.7 *Image Placement with Text*

author can reduce the size of an image and add vertical and horizontal white space around the image so that it does not appear jammed up next to the text. Figure 9.7 uses white space and a border around the image to give it some room. The example code below reduces the image size and surrounds it with 10 pixels of white space horizontally (hspace) and vertically (vspace). There is a 2-pixel border.

```
<img src="book.gif" align=top width=50 height=50 hspace=20 vspace=20 border=4
```

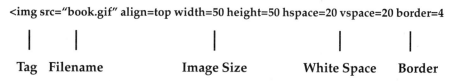

Tag   Filename   Image Size   White Space   Border

Background Images. A gif or jpeg image can also become a background image. Typically, the full monitor size is 640 by 480 pixels. Figure 9.8 compares image sizes to the way they can be used for a particular Web page format.

Pixel Dimensions	Size Description	Application
100 x 100	Custom size	Thumbnail for all formats
640 x 480	VGA (full screen)	Background image for table format Web page
800 x 600	SVGA (full screen)	Background image for table or list format Web page
1024 x 768	Full-color palette	Background for a running list format Web page

FIGURE 9.8 *Image Sizes*

FIGURE 9.9 *Tiled Background*

However, if you want to create wallpaper for the background, you would select a smaller image to use a tile, or repeating pattern. Figure 9.9 illustrates the pattern achieved by using tiles.

Web authors like tiled backgrounds to add texture and style to their pages. The name of the organization, the title of the set of Web pages, or a suitable image can be tiled against the background to simulate a watermark on fine stationery. To check the loading operation of a Web page or to add drama to the display, authors often use a background color in conjunction with a background image. If memory space is small, some authors call in a background from a source like Netscape which has freely available images. There are two backgrounds in the following example. The first is a solid-color, bright red background that adds drama and indicates that the page is loading. The second background is the tiled indian image.

<body bgcolor="ff0000" background="indian.gif">
| | |
Body Tag   Loads a Red Background Color   Loads Background Image

The HTML code changes to accommodate the location of the background image (Figure 9.10). Shortlist 30 includes sources for background images.

SHORTLIST 30
Background Images Sources

Netscape
http://www.netscape.com/assist/net_sites/backgrounds.html

MBH textures
http://www.mbh.org/texture.land/

Location	Explanation	HTML Code
floppy drive	Small graphic files loading in conjunction with Web page files on the local drive	<body background="unicorn.gif">
hard drive	Large graphic files loading in conjunction with Web page files on the local drive	<body background="authoring/ unicorn.gif">
Internet	Background loads into a Web page from its home URL	<body background="http://www. clarity.edu/~gentry/winged.gif">

FIGURE 9.10 *Background Image Codes*

SPECIAL ELEMENTS

Tables

Tables organize complex or cross-referenced information. Currently both Netscape and Internet Explorer support a table, a matrix of rows and columns. The intersection of a column and a row is a **cell**. Tables offer an excellent opportunity to compare data or to organize complex data for recall. A table can be fancy or plain. It can have a border, white space between the border and the text elements, and white space between the cells themselves. Figure 9.11 includes elements and their descriptions.

Data Set. Because data is raw information that needs to be organized and evaluated, determining how it should be presented is an art. Planning and organizing the display of raw data to best suit a target audience's needs should follow a logical course of thinking. For example, the XYZ Symphony will perform on three Saturdays at 8 p.m. at the Irving Arts Center's Carpenter Performance Hall. These performances are:

January 25, 1997	Slaussen Brothers will play the Saxophone Concerto
February 15, 1997	Amber Wittenstein will play the Theme from Star Wars
March 22, 1997	Taylor Carbone will lead the orchestra in a Tribute to the U.S. Flag

	Column	
	Row	CELL

Element	Description
border	Surrounds the perimeter of the table; measured in pixels
cellpadding	Number of pixels between cell border and text
cellspacing	Number of pixels between cells
table width = n	Table width expressed in number of pixels
table width = %	Table width expressed in percentage of page width
th	Table heading
th align = left	Table heading aligned left (center and right also codes)
th width	Table heading width can be expressed in pixels or %
th rowspan = n	Number of rows for heading
th colspan = n	Number of columns for heading

FIGURE 9.11 *Table Elements*

What kind of table will best present this information to potential concert-goers who visit the XYZ Symphony's Web site?

Table Planning Strategy. The simple table (Figure 9.12) contains three columns (date, guest artist, featured selection) and four rows with the first row containing the table's headings (date, guest artist, and featured selection). Finally, a table border of 5 pixels encloses the table and the table title is

Performance Schedule		
Date	**Guest Artist**	**Featured Selection**
Jan. 25, 1997	Slaussen Brothers	Saxophone Concerto
Feb. 15, 1997	Amber Wittenstein	Theme from Star Wars
Mar. 22, 1997	Taylor Carbone	Tribute to the U.S. Flag

FIGURE 9.12 *Concert Schedule Table*

```
<center>
<table border = 5 width=75% cellpadding=20 cellspacing=20>
    <caption align=top><font size=4><b>Performance Schedule</b></font>
    </caption>
<tr align=center>
    <th>Date</th><th>Guest Artist</th><th>Featured Selection</th>
</tr>
<tr align=center>
    <th>Jan. 25, 1997</th><td>Slaussen Brothers</td><td>Saxophone
    Concerto
    </td>
</tr>
<tr align=center>
    <th>Feb. 15, 1997</th><td>Amber Wittenstein</td><td>Theme from Star
    Wars</td>
</tr>
<tr align=center>
    <th>Mar. 22, 1997</th><td>Taylor Carbone</td><td>Tribute to the U.S.
    Flag</td>
</tr>
</table>
</center>
```

FIGURE 9.13 *Code for a Table*

centered in bold typeface. Figure 9.13 shows the HTML code for making this table.

Tables visually associate data for cross-referencing. As a grid, they segment information so that any of the table elements can also be a link by adding the codes <a href></a>. Not only do well-designed tables provide a shortcut to explanation, they also aid memory recall.

Forms

As a means of feedback and also a document of transaction, Web authors make forms that prompt response. A form is a template meant to be used over and over again. To successfully code a form, you need to have access to the CGI area, which requires special permission and manipulation by the Web administrator on the Web server. To make a form, you may use an editor or you may create the code yourself. Figure 9.14 shows a form for alumni to reply to questions about their educational experience and Figure 9.15 shows the HTML code.

Clarity University Alumni Feedback Form

Enter your Name

Enter your Address

Enter Graduation Date

Name the area of the country in which you now reside.
- ☐ East
- ☐ North
- ☐ South
- ☐ West

Gender
o Male   o Female

Please tell us how we can help you!

Please send me the following materials.

| catalog |
| alumni directory |
| membership packet |

| Submit |

FIGURE 9.14 *Alumni Feedback Form*

Style Sheets

An important consideration in future Web page design are **style sheets**. Style sheets define the structure of documents whether they are presented as Web pages or printed manuscript pages. Taken together as a module embedded in

```
<font size=6>Clarity University Alumni Feedback Form</font><p>
<hr>
<form action=http://www.clarity.edu/cgi-bin/anon.cgi method="post">
Enter your Name <input type="text" name="alumni"><p>
Enter your Address<input type="text" name="address" size="70"><p>
Enter Graduation Date <input type="text" name="date" size="10"><p>
<p>
Name the area of the country in which you now reside.<br>
<ul>
<li><input type="checkbox" name="east">East
<li><input type="checkbox" name="north">North
<li><input type="checkbox" name="south">South
<li><input type="checkbox" name="west">West
</ul>
<p>
Gender <br>
<input type="radio" name="sex" value="M">Male
<input type="radio" name="sex" value="F">Female
<p>
Please tell us how we can help you!<br>
<textarea name="comments" cols="60"></textarea>
<p>
Please send me the following materials:<br>
<select name="materials" multiple>
<option>catalog
<option>alumni directory
<option>membership packet
</select>
<p><inputtype="submit">
</form>
```

FIGURE 9.15 *Code for Alumni Feedback Form*

the source code of an HTML page, a style sheet can specify font size, special characters, and paragraph aspects all in a block of information that can be used by a single Web page or linked to several Web pages. The standard for style sheets is emerging from the initial Cascading Style Sheet experimentation at CERN in 1994, and some Web authors find the technique advantageous. Essentially style sheets set formats in blocks of code. Figure 9.16 provides an example of a style definition that appears in the <head> portion of a Web page and Shortlist 31 contains the style guide for style sheets.

```
<html><head><title>Clarity Alumni Page</title>    begins the head portion
<style>                                            begins style block

        body {font: 10 point Arial; color: 003300}    10 pt dark green body text in Arial font
        a:link {font: 12 point Arial; color: ff0000}   12 pt red active link in Arial font
        a:visited {font: 12 point Arial; color: 0000ff}  12 pt blue visited link in Arial font
        h1 {font: 36pt Arial; color: ffcc00}          36 pt gold heading 1 in Arial font
        h2 {font: 30pt Arial; color: 333300}          30 pt brown heading 2 in Arial font
</style>                                            ends style block
</head>                                             ends head portion
```

FIGURE 9.16 *Style Sheet Code*

SHORTLIST 31
Style Sheet Standard

Web Style Sheets
http://www.w3.org/style

STORYBOARDING

Storyboarding is a technique to put together pictures and text to develop the storyline of cartoons, movies, and TV shows. Today, we find that storyboarding can be an effective way to generate content for Web pages. Because content includes both text and graphics, storyboarding is a creative means to weigh visual elements against verbal elements to see if they fit together. In the following example, a student decides to describe how to read poetry and follows four steps.

1. Determine a subject and develop a mind map to establish discussion areas.
2. For the discussion areas, prepare a topical outline
   Subject: Reading Poetry
   Topical Outline: Definition of Poetry
                      Variety of Poetical Works
                      Parts of Poetry

Form—Open and Closed
Sound
Voice
Words—Choice and Implication
Rhythm—Meter, Stresses, Pauses
Imagery

3. For each topic, sketch a map of the content by starting with the topic and a thematic sentence. Consider the possibilities of information you might include and roughly lay out the information on the page, including links to other sites and any special effects or graphical elements that should be part of the content (Figure 9.17).

4. Establish a file naming convention so that each page in your project will have logical names to show a hierarchy of content (avoid the overused index.htm). See Figure 9.18.

Topic: Definition of Poetry

Thematic sentence: Poetry implies more than it expresses as it conveys an experience, offers advice, or reveals human nature.

Poetry?

Special effects:

Definition in a block.

Gif image with book pages turning

Experience [Links to William Blake's poetry]
Advice [Links to Robert Frost's poetry]
Human Nature [Links to Shakespeare's sonnets]

Background: parchment texture with black body text, blue links, red active links, purple visited links

Return to my home page.

FIGURE 9.17 *Mapping Web Page Content*

Content	Page Description	Filename
Definition of Poetry	Kathy Allen's Poetry Page	POEThome.htm
Variety of Poetical Works	Poetical Variety	POETvari.htm
Parts of Poetry	Parts of Poetry	POETpart.htm
Form	Form of Poetry	POETform.htm
Open	Open Form	FORMopen.htm
Closed	Closed Form	FORMclos.htm
Sound	Sound in Poetry	POETsoun.htm
Voice	Voice in Poetry	POETvoic.htm
Words	Words in Poetry	POETword.htm
Choice	Word Choice	WORDchoi.htm
Implication	Word Implication	WORDimpl.htm
Rhythm	Rhythm in Poetry	POETrhym.htm
Meter	Rhythm and Meter	RHYMmetr.htm
Stresses	Rhythm and Stresses	RHYMstre.htm
Pauses	Rhythm and Pauses	RHYMpaus.htm
Imagery	Imagery in Poetry	POETimag.htm

FIGURE 9.18 *Logical File Naming*

Through the Looking Glass

The following exercises allow you to explore and draw conclusions about what you see; in essence, you get to be the expert.

WEB LINGO

animated images   cell

bandwidth   dithering

Graphics Interchange
  Format (gif)
grayscale
image maps
inline images
interlacing
Joint Photographic Experts
  Group (jpeg or jpg)

live connection
style sheets
thumbnail
transparent
watermark

WEB ITINERARY

1. Use a search engine to find out about your family's history and geneaology. Prepare a Web page that describes your family tree and its branches.
2. For a club or organization you belong to, prepare a series of Web pages that describe its purpose and structure. Use a table format Web page to create icons that link to the following Web pages. Create a form for prospective members to get information, and a page of hypertext links to sites related to your organization.
3. Critique the Web pages designed by a peer, remembering to give fair and constructive suggestions. Offer a list of a few Web sites that may have the same subject matter and share with your peer a list of Web sites that have an appealing design.
4. To maintain an orderly system of HTML coding, Web authors adhere to HTML standards. Undertake a research project to find out which is the currently adopted HTML standard and the presently drafted standard. Write an essay in which you describe the differences between the two standards.
5. Internet Explorer and Netscape are constantly refining their browsers. Write an exploratory essay in which you predict how browsers will change. Use examples and evidence from the Web.

PROJECT ASSIGNMENT

Travel to some virtual museums to evaluate how they landscape text with graphics to show and tell about something. Notice the special effects and user convenience features. Create your own museum by collecting artifacts from the Web that interest you. Use thumbnail images as links to referenced URLs holding the artifacts.

Here is the source code for an advanced page that uses a table format with two columns. The first column functions as a table of contents that links to information in the second column, which is organized as a list format. The source code begins with a prologue <!DOCTYPE...> which specifies that this is a public document for the WWW. The code includes comment lines <!--...--> to describe parts of the code.

```
<!DOCTYPE HTML PUBLIC "-//W3C//DTD HTML
3.2//EN"><HTML><HEAD><TITLE>Your Name's Museum
Page</TITLE></HEAD>

<BODY TEXT="#ffff00" BGCOLOR="#0F0F8F" LINK="#FF0033"
VLINK="#0099CC" ALINK="#003366" left margin="0"
TOPMARGIN="0"><P><font size=6>Your Name's Museum</font>
<!--begin split column-->
<A NAME="top"></A><BR><!--sets a page anchor-->
<TABLE CELLSPACING=0 CELLPADDING=4 BGCOLOR="#fff8dc"
text="#3366ff" link="#054BfB" vlink="#006342" ><TR><TD width=124
valign=top><A NAME="top"></A>
<P>CONTENTS<P>
<TT><A HREF="#modern">Modern Works</A></font><BR><!--sets a
link to modern works-->
<A HREF="#renaiss">Renaissance Masterpieces</A><BR><!--sets a link to
Renaissance works-->
<A HREF="#ancient">Ancient Artifacts</A><br><!--sets a link to ancient
works-->
<A HREF="#sources">Sources</A><br><!--sets a link to the source list-->
<!--go to second column-->
<TD width=375 valign=top cellspacing=5 cellpadding=0 border="#992200"
bgcolor="#0F0F8F" text="#ffff00"><BR>
<center><P><b><font size=4>Your Name</font></b><br><font
size=3><b>Your University</font></b></center><P>
<font size=6>H</font><font size=4>ere is a gathering of works like the
<font size=5><A
HREF="http://www.comlab.ox.ac.uk/archive/other/museums/
world.html">Virtual Museums</a>.<P>
<center><font size=4><a name="modern">Modern
Works</a></font></center><p>
```
Write your own commentary about modern works and include images.<p>

<font size=4><a name="renaiss">Renaissance Masterpieces</a> <p>
Write your own commentary about Renaissance Masterpieces and include images.<p>
<font size=4><a name="ancient">Ancient Artifacts</a> <p>
Write your own commentary about Ancient Artifacts and include images.<p>
<font size=1><a href="URL">Return to . . ..</a></font><!--list your institution's home page or your own-->
<P> <FONT SIZE=-1>Copyright © 1997 Lory Hawkes, Ph.D.
All rights reserved</font>
<hr size=4><address><font size=2>For more information, please e-mail: <a href="mailto: account@college.edu">Your Name.</a></font></address> </TD></TR></TABLE>
</BODY>
</HTML>

CHAPTER 10
Dreamscapes & Experiments

Academic Experiments
Commercial Experiments
Virtual Worlds

> *Earth in the next century will have its collective consciousness lifted off the planet's surface into a dense electronic symphony where all nations— if they still exist as separate entities—may live in a clutch of spontaneous synesthesia, painfully aware of the triumphs and wounds of one another.*
>
> THE GLOBAL VILLAGE

ACADEMIC EXPERIMENTS

The Web is a laboratory for new experimentation in designing visually appealing hypertext documents that use language and images to create visions of the real world and of the surreal world. Two ambitious experiments by the Michigan Institute of Technology's Media Lab are important as studies of the social construction of knowledge using contributions from Web users. On October 10, 1995, the first experiment was held as a tribute to the decade-long existence of the lab. Aptly named *A Day in the Life of Cyberspace*, this undertaking invited the Web's global audience to submit pictures, sounds, and written expressions to be combined digitally and presented to the world as a representation of a digital renaissance. Although the lab's developers wanted to collect artifacts and reexhibit them on the Web, their ambitious study yielded much more than a simple collection. Dividing the wealth of the contributions into a portrait gallery and a narrative archive, the lab in effect created a dreamscape that provided real and surreal visions of cyberspace. People told about their experiences and attempted to show what the experiences meant to them. Moreover, by effectively associating language and images in a compelling state-of-the-art Web site, the lab developed a site that combined commentary and images to ultimately create an art form.

Building on the success and critical acclaim of its first venture, the lab attempted a second, the *Brain Opera*. Again inviting suggestions from the global audience about the kinds of music to include, noted composer Tod Machover and the lab developers designed an interactive musical program that was given in free performances in Lincoln Center during the summer of 1996 and that included contributions from online users as well. Against a dramatic solid black backdrop, a human brain appeared to play music—using the multimedia aspects of the Internet, the lab depicted a dreamscape of human thought process as it encounters music and sound. Shortlist 32 contains outstanding academic experiments, some of which may no longer be available.

SHORTLIST 32
Academic Experiments

MIT Brain Opera
http://brainop.medi.mit.edu

MIT Day in the Life of Cyberspace
http://www.1010.org

MIT Design Interaction Paradigms
http://design-paradigms.www.media.mit.edu/projects/design-paradigms

MIT Gesture and Narrative Language
http://gn.www.media.mit.edu/groups/gn/

Georgia Tech's Graphics, Visualization, and Usability Center
http://www.cc.gatech.edu/gvu/gvutop.html

COMMERCIAL EXPERIMENTS

Types of Sites

As corporations and organizations move their information on the Web, three categories of sites appear: promotional, content, and transaction. The **promotional site** conveys information about an organization to build credibility and public awareness. This site is usually a forerunner of the second category, the content site. The **content site** provides more in-depth information about an organization and may entertain users with games or simulations of their product or company. Automobile manufacturers have content sites that give potential customers product information and a few allow users to test-drive their vehicles. The third category is the **transaction site** that establishes a favorable public presence, provides in-depth information and some interactive entertainment, and enables customers to buy products. Both Netscape and Microsoft are good examples of transaction sites.

Building and maintaining these sites are expensive. Forrester Research projected figures into 1997 that show the promotional site as the cheapest of the three at a total cost for start-up, service, and marketing equal to well over half a million dollars. The total for a content site is just shy of two million dollars, while the cost for a transaction site is over four million (Figure 10.1). Compared to 1995, the costs in each category almost doubled by 1997 (Mullich 37). Because of the escalating expense of building and maintaining Web information, media and entertainment firms lead the way in underwriting visually provocative Web sites.

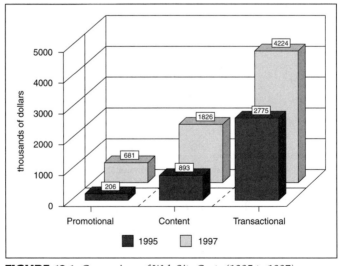

FIGURE 10.1 *Comparison of Web Site Costs (1995 to 1997)*

Pacesetter Sites

MTV stands out as an innovator in digital art and expression and maintains a successful content site. MTV's home page's centerpiece is a single three-dimensional letter M jutting out from a pitch-black background.

As a transaction site, MTV builds a dreamscape that is particularly suited to its target audience. The goal is to interest Web users in the site and to inform loyal viewers about ongoing events and special features. The written expression is upbeat and direct, and the graphics and typography transport the user into another world—a bold new world of happenings.

MTV started out as an experiment in television programming, and continues setting trends on the Web. Its Web site sets a standard for entertainment sites. Its accurate information and compelling presentation invite Web users to linger and explore the site, as well as provide a source of entertainment to woo potential viewers. Similarly, the Disney Corporation has a site that contains relevant information tailored to families in an intriguing venue that projects Web users into another world. Shortlist 33 includes notable commercial experiments.

Virtual Reality Site

Evolving from the static hypertext display into a bold new world of motion, sound, and mythmaking is the final form of experimental site—the virtual world. Utopia is a dreamscape in purpose and operation. First, its purpose is to introduce Web users to the OnLive! Technologies software by immersing them in a three-dimensional fantasy world. The dreamscape extends to creations of mythical creatures called **avatars**. (A virtual environment is simulated in Figure 10.2.) The avatar can be human, animal, or surreal depending on the virtual scenario and the character that the Web user selects. These creatures can move through a scene to encounter other avatars. Adding

---

SHORTLIST 33
Commercial Experiments

MTV
http://www.mtv.com

Disney
http://www.disney.com

ByteNet's Some Experimental Sites
http://www.bytenet.co.uk/byte/bn_cuttingedge.html

FIGURE 10.2 *A Virtual World Simulation*

another dimension, the avatars actually speak to one another in real-time conversation via previously installed software using a microphone on the home computer. Voices can be real or disguised using special effects.

Transactional sites like Utopia signal an important breakthrough in the ability to construct dreamscapes with animation, colors, and sound. Movement and conversation is totally self-initiated and self-directed. Encounters with other avatars provide entertainment and adventure. Other gaming sites like Nintendo demonstrate their games in a three-dimensional virtual environment of a dreamscape to intrigue potential customers and to promote their products (Shortlist 34).

SHORTLIST 34
Three-Dimensional Virtual Environments

Alphawood
http://www.activeworld.com

Dave Central
http://www.davecentral.com

Intel's Home Page
http://www.intel.com/

Moir Brandts Honk
http://www.mbh.org/vrml/

Nintendo
http://www.thepalace.com/index.html

OnLive! Traveler
http://www.onlive.com/prod/trav

FUTURE WORLDS

Prospects for the Next Generation

Three decades ago, philosopher and soothsayer Marshall McLuhan discussed the future of television. He believed that TV could ultimately be a dreamscape in which the viewer would be involved in a synesthesia (94) or state of heightened awareness brought on by things that appeal to the senses like sight, sound, taste, smell, etc. Television may reach that state with Web TV, which attempts to join the older broadcast technology with the newer technology of Internet access. However, TV has not allowed viewers self-direction, other than changing channels. Television continues to be an audience-centered activity, with an audience of passive viewers.

The significant distinction with virtual reality environments like Utopia is that they are performance-centered, requiring the audience to interact. McLuhan's theory that technology would eventually envelope users in a sense-enhanced environment has come true in these virtual reality environments. Whether these environments will be destructive by sapping away human intellect, a prediction of many Hollywood films, or constructive by giving underprivileged individuals an opportunity to learn about the larger world outside their neighborhoods remains to be seen. Their existence does herald the dawn of a brave new world that can entice and prolong virtual interaction, and experimental sites do set a standard for future Web site development and commercial competition.

Problems for Our Generation

In ancient Greece, Aristotle advocated balance in one's life with nothing to excess. He said that the happy person was one who shared good will with others and practiced a virtuous life. There is power and financial reward in making and manipulating virtual environments. Our generation must now struggle with issues that confront us and find ethical solutions to protect those who are virtuous and to control those who are not.

Although virtual environments can open up stimulating worlds of discovery especially to those who are handicapped or unable to leave their homes, these worlds can also distract human reasoning, provide a false sense of power, and be habit forming. As technology improves our ability to communicate, it seems that communication may also be the root of societal evil. Chat-room participation has been the source of marriages breaking up; young children have been lured away from their homes by going to Web pages or responding to e-mail; people of all ages have been victims of fraudulent offers by companies whose only presence is on the Web.

Even while there have been abuses, there have also been successes. Many people can now enjoy the thrill of being self-published, the heady experience of talking with citizens from around the world, and the almost instantaneous dissemination of news and commentary about major events.

The key question for our generation seems to be: How can we balance our need to explore virtual worlds and to learn about the Web and still meet our responsibilities to our families, to our employers, and to ourselves? The way we balance our need to discover with our obligations may mean the difference between possessing technology or being possessed by it.

Through the Looking Glass

The following exercises allow you to explore and draw conclusions about what you see; in essence, you get to be the expert.

WEB LINGO

avatars

content site

promotional site

transaction site

WEB ITINERARY

1. Here are a few issues confronting businesses that deal with technology. Research one issue and create a Web page that explains the issue, provides key terms, and gives a balanced view of the controversy.

   Fraud and Mismanagement
   Government Regulation
   Monopoly
   Intellectual Property
   Profit Margins
   Scientific Inquiry
   Taxation

2. Here are a few issues confronting individuals who use the Web and technology. Research one issue and create a Web page that explains the issue, provides key terms, and gives a balanced view of the controversy.

   Exploitation and Manipulation
   Government Surveillance
   Industry Surveillance
   Personal Freedom
   Privacy

3. Here are a few issues confronting governments dealing with the Web and technology. Research one issue and create a Web page that explains the issue, provides key terms, and gives a balanced view of the controversy.

   Espionage
   International Treaties
   National Law Enforcement
   Revenue

5. There are three types of sites: promotional, content, and transaction. Use a search engine to find examples of each site and then create a Web page to discuss the purpose, scope, and organization of each type as well as give examples of each type as links.

PROJECT ASSIGNMENT

As a class, survey the people in your institution to determine the prevailing attitude toward virtual environments. Divide up the issues into topics with each person in the class creating an essay on at least one topic. Publish the essays as part of Web pages that compose a special issue of an online publication to share your findings and your writings about technological issues.

FOR FURTHER READING

McLuhan, Marshall and Bruce R. Powers. *The Global Village: Transformations in World Life and Media in the 21st Century*. Oxford: Oxford UP, 1989.
Mullich, Joe. "World Wide Web Development Sticker Shock." *Uniforum's IT Solutions* Jul. 1996: 34–37.

Miscellany

Computers will, in the long run, dramatically alter the social environment of the workplace as we know it.

THE GLOBAL VILLAGE

PATHFINDING

Finding the Root URL

If you find that an URL given in this book is no longer operational, here are a few savvy tips to help you backtrack to the root URL to find the resource. For example, the URL for Scott Rettberg's *Books in Chains* can be separated as follows:

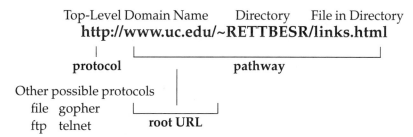

Because of the constant state of improvement within Web sites, authors may modify directory locations and file names without notice. If the browser displays an error message,

1. Edit the URL in the location box to delete a portion of the URL at a time, starting with the last element (in this case *links.html*).
2. If another search on the edited URL does not work, delete all elements except the top-level domain name and the protocol, which is known as the root URL.
3. Since top-level domains rarely change, a user may be able to follow links from the Web site's home page to the desired site.
4. If you still cannot find the site, in this case because the surname is unique, you can do a search on AltaVista or Lycos for "Rettberg" or "books in chains."

Downloading and Installing Files

Software files, especially upgrades of the popular browser programs, appear as self-extracting archives with an *.exe* extension. For example, when a program like LviewPro is downloaded, it is compressed like a dry sponge. When the program is activated by using Windows to run its .exe file, the program expands to automatically decompress all of the files necessary for the program to work properly and to fill up the directory. Any error in transmission from the download source could cause an error in the program decompression. If the directory or computer is out of memory space, the program may not be able to decompress or run. Because Netscape Navigator 4.0 and Internet Explorer 4.0 are so popular as browsers, these programs have an intermediary program to help users successfully complete the download and installation process by prompting them for decisions. Here are some tips to use to find out how to download and extract files.

Note: Unfortunately, program file names may not be self-explanatory. For instance, the beta 6 version of Netscape was g3230b6m.exe and it expands to 3, 704, 320 bytes of information. Plug-ins are software applications that work with the program. These plug-ins require additional memory space and sometimes troubleshooting to make them work properly.

1. If the source site has a FAQ, a readme file, or a link to information about downloading, read all of the information carefully. Know how much memory is required when the files are decompressed, understand the platform (MS-DOS or Macintosh), and know the size of the compressed file and estimated time of download. These specific directions take precedence over the following general advice.
2. Make a new directory on your hard drive, giving it a name that is similar to the program you intend to copy there.
3. Open your browser and travel to the source site by specifying the URL.
4. Print out important installation directions or trouble reports as a reminder about what to do after you download the file.
5. The source site will identify a process to download a file and prompt you to supply a destination on your computer. The destination should be your new directory.
6. Once the file is downloaded into the new directory, you may go to the Start menu on the Windows 95 desktop and select run, specifying the .exe file that you have just downloaded.

EXPERT HTML

Background. **Hypertext Markup Language (HTML)** is an application of **Standard Generalized Markup Language (SGML)** and the outgrowth of large-scale publishing companies to find a comprehensive way to define and routinely identify **universal components** of a document. For example, headings, paragraphs, figures, and tables could be common elements of documents and therefore considered as universal components. In the late 1960s, there were attempts to use blue-penciled codes to indicate the placement of text and graphics to guide printers and typesetters. The attempts became an initiative for **Generalized Markup Language (GML)** spearheaded by computing giant IBM in the early 1970s. In GML, the codes could be interpreted by computers processing the data so that a format could be established with typical elements like paragraphs and headings of various levels. A decade later, with the advent of word processing and improving computer technology, SGML was born and soon developed its own standard that relied on **document type definitions (DTD)** to specify the kind of document and model of informational flow, on links to bind together content and structure, and on common English tags to describe an element like a title and to show the contents of a document element like a title:

<title>Company Policy</title>

As an offspring of an extensive coding process, HTML has similar English formatting codes held in tags. Currently, there are three versions of HTML which may have a different look from browser to browser. HTML version 1.0 is official, version 2.0 is widely adopted, and version 3.0 with Netscape extensions is experimental but receiving serious attention because of its exciting potential for special effects and multimedia. If your browser accepts only HTML version 2.0, no version 3.0 elements will be processed. Consequently, the final look of the page could be different or even distorted.

Documenting Your Web Page.   In the beginning, you must say what kind of document you are creating and then give a title to the page, which in turn will be keywords that search engines read to decide what your page is about. As a standard way to mark up a page, the HTML code links a typical document element to specific content:

```
<html>
<head><title>A Guide to the World Wide Web</title>
</head>
```

When the page appears seen through a browser, the tags are not visible because they are part of the **source code**. Although the source code in the following examples may appear with blocks of text and indented statements, the source code is processed by the server as a **data stream** or said another way, like a single line of text.

An optional item, which some Web developers recommend before the head element, is a comment line that specifies the document type based on the HTML version being used. Although the comment line <!--   --> would not be visible outside the source code, it would give other Web developers viewing your source code important information. This kind of comment is called a **prologue,** and it describes a public HTML document intended for the Web that uses HTML version 3.0. The prologue roughly translated identifies the page as a public document using the W3C World Wide Web convention in the HTML 3.0 standard.

```
<!--doctype html public "-//W3C//DTD W3 HTML 3.0//EN"-->
<html><head><title>A Guide to the World Wide Web</title></head>
```

An alternate form for a prologue to help professors quickly identify student work is:

```
<!--Bobby Smith, Sociology 425-003-->
<!--College Name, date-->
<html><head><title>Bobby Smith's White Paper</title></head>
```

A powerful new tag, the **meta**, is in the Head portion of an HTML file. The meta tag can convey descriptive information about the document or alert users that the expiration date is near. A meta tag can also be used to embed commands to the browser to operate under certain conditions. If you use a Web page editor, the editor puts in a meta tag indicating the name of the editor. Authors use meta tags to denote the format, to supply keywords for search engines to categorize the site, and to send and receive a cookie (a file stored on your computer to gather information about your preferences and to be sent back to the company when you visit their site again). Although both Netscape Navigator and Internet Explorer allow users to set the browser preferences or security to intercept cookies and prompt to accept or reject them, Internet Explorer makes it a requirement that the user agree to accept cookies as a condition of getting its free browser. Figure M.1 contains codes for meta tags.

Frames.   A frame is a container for other material held in separate windows. A Web page divided by frames is like a picture frame with a mat that has cutouts for several smaller pictures. Each of the cutouts become an inner frame that contains a different picture. Each picture can be seen in relation to an adjacent picture or in relation to the whole set of pictures in the outer frame.

A frame document consists of information that is grouped into separate inner frames which are logically related to one another. Newer browsers like Netscape Navigator 4 and Internet Explorer 4 correctly display frame documents. Older versions of both browsers (2.0 and under) do not.

In order to determine whether your information is suitable for a frame document, you need to look at the extent of information to see if it can be divided and then classified. Suppose you have a picture of Shakespeare and

Description	Tag
Hypertext file with a specific character set	<meta http-equiv= "Content-Type" character set content="text/html; charset= iso-8859-1>
Characterizes the contents of the meta name "author"	<meta name="author" content="Barry Smith">
Characterizes the contents of the meta name "keywords"	<meta name="keywords" content="online, help,Web, Internet, writing">
Attributes the creation of the document to Netscape HTML	<meta name="generator" content="Mozilla/ 4.0b5 [en] (Win95: I) [Netscape]">

FIGURE M.1 *Meta Tag Codes*

you want to show a list of his works linked to other Web sites. You could put Shakespeare's picture in one frame and the list in another frame. As the designer, you would have to decide the logical relationship: should the frames be stacked on one another or should they be side by side?

For example, let's say we have two files (file1.htm and file2.htm). The first file has a picture of Shakespeare in it and the second file has the list of bookmarks to his works. To set the frame layout for the two files, you would have to compose a frameset file to describe how they will appear in proximity to each other. The frameset statement substitutes for the body statement in your frameset Web page. In order to stack the picture (file1.htm) on top of the bookmark list (file2.htm), you would create a frameset statement like this:

```
<frameset cols="50%,50%">
```

File1.htm
File2.htm

In other words, you are taking 100 percent of the display area of the browser and dividing it into two halves. Another way to compose the frameset statement is to place the files side by side:

```
<frameset rows="50%,50%">
```

You've taken the same 100 percent of the display area of the browser and you have divided that space into two blocks that are side by side.

File1.htm	File2.htm

Now let's see how the last arrangement into side-by-side blocks would look in a frameset file.

Beginning tags	`<html><head><title>Frame Page Example</title></head>`
Frameset statement	`<frameset rows="50%,50%">`
Source of the	`<frame src="file1.htm">`
content	`<frame src="file2.htm">`
	`</frameset>`
Ending tags	`</html>`

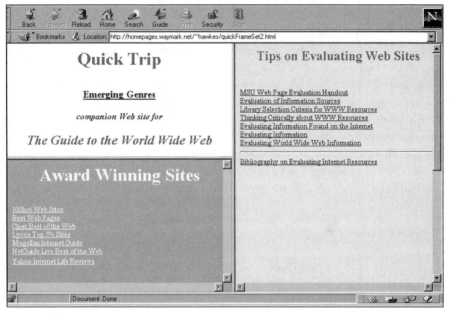

FIGURE M.2 *Frames Web Page*

To design the Web page in Figure M.2 there are four files. The file with the title Quick Trip (upper left) is quicktrip.html; the file with the list of award-winning sites (bottom left) is quick1.html; and the file with tips on evaluating sites (right) is quick2.html. These files are simple and their HTML codes will not be shown. However, because the key to properly laying out the files is the frameset file called quickset.html, Figure M.3 lists the HTML code.

In figure M.3, you see a prologue, followed by the head portion of the HTML file. Instead of a body statement, there is a frameset statement that sets up the two columns, <frameset cols>. Next an embedded frameset statement sets up two rows in the first column, <frameset rows>. Indention in the code helps to show the way that a <frameset rows> statement is embedded after the <frameset cols> statement. To help the user of this document, a <no frames> warning is the only visible text in this file and therefore a body statement is included. Figure M.4 has an explanation of layout codes.

Java.   When Sun Microsystems and Netscape introduced **Java** scripting, it marked an important event. As a subset of C++, Java is a language that imbues an object with behaviors. For example, a star can twinkle, twirl, and slide across the Web page because a Java script charts its path, its change of colors, and its speed from one coordinate to another. As a common language, Java code is translatable from one platform to another. A star sliding across a

```
<!–doctype html public "-//W3C//DTD W3 HTML 3.0//EN"–>
<HTML>
<HEAD><TITLE>Guide to WWW_Quick Trip</TITLE></HEAD>

<FRAMESET COLS="59%,41%">
   <FRAMESET ROWS="58%,42%">
    <FRAME SRC="quicktrip.html" SCROLLING=NO>
    <FRAME SRC="quick1.html" SCROLLING=YES>
    </FRAMESET><FRAME SRC="quick2.html SCROLLING=YES>
<NOFRAMES>
<BODY>
Viewing this page requires a browser capable of displaying frames.
</BODY>
</NO FRAMES>
</FRAMESET>
</HTML>
```

FIGURE M.3 *Frameset HTML Code*

Description	Tag
Identifies the size and shape of the document in numbers meaning pixels or in percentages <frameset rows="200, 150, 250"> pixels *Note: rows are 200 pixels, 150 pixels and 250 pixels tall* <frameset cols= "30%, 30%, 40%"> *column percentages exactly equal 100%; when the percentage is not 100%, the browser will resize in proportion to accommodate the indicated dimensions*	<frameset rows="#", cols="#">
Content is held in a source file	<frame src="filename.htm">
Name gives the frame an alternate name that can be used later to call it up	<name="frame1">
Noresize holds and freezes the dimensions of the frame	<noresize>
Scrolling allows content to move up and down within the frame in reaction to a slide bar movement	<scrolling=yes>
Noframes warning if browser cannot display frames	<noframes>

FIGURE M.4 *Frame Layout Codes*

Web page on a computer using a Microsoft Windows platform will act the same way on a Macintosh computer. Java script uses the applet tag in HTML and typically goes between the <head></head> tags. An applet is a block of codes that define the behavior of an object. Although Netscape requires coding of Java script for object movement, Internet Explorer offers a Marquee feature that causes your word or phrase to scroll across the screen. Because Java requires more advanced programming knowledge to understand its models, no examples are given in this short discussion.

Multimedia.   **Sound** and **video** clips can be added to a Web page for drama or authenticity, provided the HTML code is compatible with the browser and the file format is correct. The discussion in this book does not assume that you are building a Web page that anticipates the browser type and then selects the correct code to play the sound, so it does not cover streaming audio that requires an embedded plug-in. Streaming audio means that a player initiates the recorded sound which continues until the sound is finished or until you turn off the player. You may need to use a Java script to accomplish this process. This discussion does give simple commands that help you include sound and video in your Web page.

Standard extensions for sound files are: *.au* and *.wav*. Other sound formats include: *.rp* or *.rpm, .dsp, .mp2*. Netscape Navigator 4.0 handles the sound file dance.wav as a hypertext link in conjunction with the image of a dancer.

```
<a href="dance.wav"><img src="dancer.gif ALT="waltz"></a>
```

Internet Explorer 4.0 associates a background sound with a page. In addition, loop statements permit the sound clip to play indefinitely (loop=infinite) or a specified number of times (loop=2)

```
<bgsound src="dance.wav" loop=2>
```

Video files, like sound files, take up memory space and appear in a tag within the body of the document. Three formats of video files have these extensions: *.mpeg, .mov* (Quick Time), and *.avi* (Video for Windows). The Netscape code to make the image punkrock.jpg a link to the Quick Time movie called funky.mov is:

```
<a href="funky.mov"><img src="punkrock.jpg" ALT="[punkrock]">.
```

In Internet Explorer 4.0, the video file is a dynamic source and therefore this code plays an .avi movie

```
<img dynsrc="joker.avi">
```

Sound and video files can also be specified as a frame source in a frame document.

NETSCAPE NAVIGATOR 4.0

The following pages give a quick reference to the operational features of Netscape Navigator 4.0, which is based on the early CERN interface. If you have purchased the Netscape program, refer to your accompanying reference manual for differences between the previous version 3.0 and this newer version. To download the free version of Netscape Navigator 4.0 that is operational for 60 days, travel to Netscape's home page at http://home.netscape. com. Follow the directions there to download the latest version. Figures M.5 and M.6 show the menu and screen organization of Netscape Navigator.

Title Bar and Menu Bar
Title Bar   Displays the currently retrieved document's Web page title
Menu Bar   Gives a list of menu options, which have these submenu options
Tool Bar   Helpful buttons to perform the most common tasks

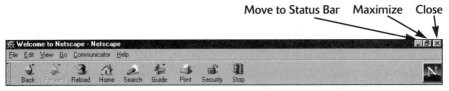

FIGURE M.5 *Netscape's Menu*

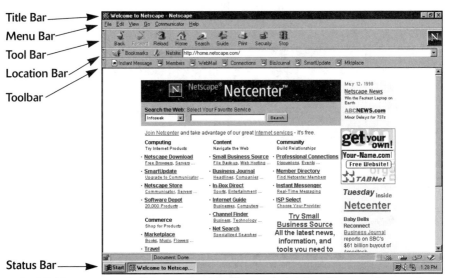

FIGURE M.6 *Netscape Full Screen. Reprinted by permission from Netscape Communications Corporation, 1997. All rights reserved. Netscape, Netscape Navigator, and the Netscape N logo are registered trademarks of Netscape in the United States and other countries.*

File	Edit	View	Go	Communicator	Help
New	Cut	Navigation Toolbar	Back	Navigator	Help Contents
Open Page	Copy	Location Toolbar	Forward	Messenger Mailbox	Release Notes
Save As	Paste	Personal Toolbar	Home	Collabra Discussion Groups	Product Info & Support
Save Frame	Select All	Increase Font	Welcome	Page Composer	Software Updates
Send Page	Find in Page	Decrease Font		Conference	Register Now
Edit Page	Find Again	Reload		Component Bar	Member Services
Edit Frame	Search Internet	Show Images		Message Center	International Users
Upload File	Search Directory	Refresh		Address Book	Security
Go Offline	Preferences	Stop Page Loading		Bookmarks	Net Etiquette
Page Setup		Stop Animation		History	About Plug-ins
Print Preview		Page Source		Java Console	About Font Displays
Print		Page Info		Security Info	About Communicator
Close		Page Services		Welcome	
Exit		Encoding			

FIGURE M.7 *Netscape Navigator 4.0 Commands*

Netscape ShortCut	Description	Internet Explorer ShortCut	Description
CTRL A	Select All	CTRL A	Select All
CTRL B	Edit Bookmark		
CTRL C	Copy	CTRL C	Copy
CTRL D	Add Bookmark		
CTRL E			
CTRL F	Find in Page	CTRL F	Find
CTRL G	Find Again		
CTRL H	History		
CTRL O	Open Page	CTRL O	Open
CTRL P	Print	CTRL P	Print
CTRL Q	Quit		
CTRL R	Reload		
CTRL S	Save	CTRL S	Save
CTRL U	Page Source		
CTRL V	Paste	CTRL V	Paste
CTRL W	Close		
CTRL X	Cut	CTRL X	Cut
CTRL 1	Navigator		
CTRL 2	Messenger Mailbox		
CTRL 3	Collabra Discussion Group		
CTRL 4	Page Composer		
CTRL 5	Conference		
CTRL SFT 1	Message Center		
CTRL SFT 2	Address Book		
CTRL SFT I	Security Info		
CTRL]	Increase Font		
CTRL [	Decrease Font		
		F5	Refresh
ESC	Stop	ESC	Stop

FIGURE M.8 *Netscape Navigator/Internet Explorer Shortcut Keys*

INTERNET EXPLORER 4.0

Internet Explorer 4.0 is based on the early Mosaic browser which many educational institutions and the National Science Foundation used to explore the Internet. According to Microsoft, Internet Explorer will always be offered for free download. If you have bought Microsoft Windows 95, you may already have Internet Explorer because the browser is bundled with the Windows and Office programs. To download Internet Explorer travel to the Microsoft home page at http://www.microsoft.com. Follow the directions to get the program.

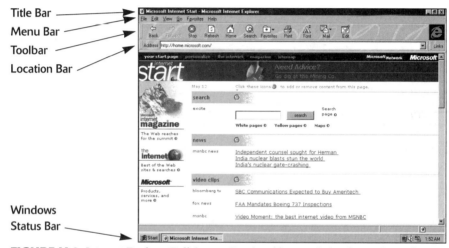

FIGURE M.9 *Internet Explorer Full Screen. Reprinted by permission from Microsoft Corporation.*

File	Edit	View	Go	Favorites	Help
New	Cut	Toolbars	Back	Add to Favorites	Contents & Index
Open	Copy	Status Bar	Forward	Organize Favorites	Product Updates
Save	Paste	Explorer Bar	Up One Level	Manage Subscriptions	Web Tutorial
Save As	Select All	Fonts	Home Page	Update All Subscriptions	Online Support
Page Setup	Page	Stop	Channel Guide	Channels	Microsoft on the Web

FIGURE M.10 *Internet Explorer 4.0 Commands (continued next page)*

Print	Find	Refresh	Search the Web	Imported Bookmarks	About Internet Explorer
Send		Source	Mail	Links	
Properties		Full Screen	My Computer	Software Update	
Internet Start		Internet Options	Address Book	My Documents	
Internet Guide					

FIGURE M.10 *(cont.)*

TAG	MEANING	EXAMPLE
a	Anchor signifies a hypertext link	**\<a href="filename.htm"\>**
b	Boldface	**\<b\>\</b\>**
bgsound src (ie)	Inserts a background sound from the URL	**\<bgsound src="sigh.wav"\>**
	for .wav, .au, or .mid files	
blockquote	Indents a block of text from left	**\<blockquote\>\</blockquote\>**
body	Sets apart the visible text area of a hyperdocument	**\<body\>\</body\>**
br	Line break to stop a line of text and wrap to next line of text	**\<br\>**
caption	Text that titles a table	**\<caption\>\</caption\>**
dd	Sets apart text that is a definition within a definition list, used as a tab for text	**\<dd\>\</dd\>**
dl	Begins and ends a definition list	**\<dl\>\</dl\>**
dt	Sets out a term in a definition list	**\<dt\>\</dt\>**
em	Emphasizes the text	**\<em\>\</em\>**
font font color font face (ie4)	Regulates font size Regulates font color Specifies a typestyle like Times Roman	**\<font size = 3\>\</font\>** **\<font color="blue"\>\</font\>** **\<font face="Times"\>\</font\>**
form	Sets apart a form	**\<form\>\</form\>**
frame	Sets apart the description of how the hyperdocument will be divided into panes	**\<frame\>\</frame\>**
frameset	Describes how the frame will be pictured	**\<frameset\>\</frameset\>**
h	Determines the size and boldness of a heading (h1 is biggest and boldest, h6 is smallest and least bold)	**\<h1\>\</h1\>**

FIGURE M.11 *Common HTML Codes for Netscape and Internet Explorer (continued on next page)*

TAG	MEANING	EXAMPLE
hr	Places a horizontal rule; hr in conjunction with a size statement makes the rule thicker, like <hr size=5>	<hr>
html	Defines the document as a hypertext markup language document; inserted at the beginning and end of all code	<html></html>
img src dynsrc (ie)	Describes and calls up an image Specifies the URL of the video (AVI file)	<img src="filename.gif"> <dynsrc="renais.avi">
input	Sets out how data will be given by the user in a form	<input>
li	Defines a listed item in an ordered list with a sequential number or in an unordered list with a bullet	<li>
marquee (ie)	Makes scrolling or sliding text appear	<marquee></marquee>
meta	Advanced feature for both browsers that enables manipulation of browser displays; appears in the head portion	<meta>
nobr	Stops a line from breaking	<nobr>
ol	Defines an ordered list with numbered list items	<ol></ol>
p	Paragraph serves as a double line break	<p>
pre	Preformatted text from a word-processed document is put in as is	<pre></pre>
strong	Emphasizes text by making it bold	<strong></strong>
table	Sets out a table and ends it within the body portion	<table></table>
title	Defines the title of the document in the head portion	<title></title>
u	Underscores text	<u></u>
ul	Sets out an unordered list with bulleted list items	<ul></ul>

FIGURE M.11 *Common HTML Codes for Netscape and Internet Explorer (cont.)*

LISTS

Domestic and International Domain Names

Being able to predict the location and type of Web site from a URL allows users to plan their Web excursions. For quick reference, the three-character domain designations for most sites in the United States are listed in Figure M.12; Figure M.13 lists international domain designations.

Domain Designation	Description
com	For corporations, commercial firms, and industry
edu	For universities and institutions devoted to education
gov	For government organizations excluding the military
mil	For the U.S. military and its agencies
net	For miscellaneous organizations and networks
org	For professional and other organizations falling outside of previous domains

FIGURE M.12 *Domestic Domain Names*

Domain	Country	Domain	Country
uk	United Kingdom	sg	Singapore
de	Germany	cz	Czech Republic
jp	Japan	ru	Russian Federation
us	United States (rarely used)	tw	Taiwan
ca	Canada	hu	Hungary
au	Australia	hk	Hong Kong
fi	Finland	ie	Ireland
nl	Netherlands	mx	Mexico
fr	France	pt	Portugal
se	Sweden	cl	Chile
no	Norway	gr	Greece
it	Italy	cn	China
ch	Switzerland	is	Iceland
za	South Africa	si	Slovenia
nz	New Zealand	ar	Argentina
dk	Denmark	my	Malaysia
at	Austria	tr	Turkey
es	Spain	ee	Estonia
kr	Republic of Korea	th	Thailand
br	Brazil	sk	Slovak Republic
be	Belgium	co	Colombia
il	Israel	id	Indonesia
pl	Poland	ua	Ukraine

FIGURE M.13 *International Domain Names from Largest to Smallest Number of Hosts (1996) (continued on next page)*

Domain	Country	Domain	Country
ph	Philippines	li	Liechtenstein
lv	Latvia	ke	Kenya
lu	Luxembourg	mo	Macau
ro	Romania	ge	Georgia
cr	Costa Rica	am	Armenia
hr	Croatia	by	Belarus
pe	Peru	mc	Monaco
bg	Bulgaria	mk	Macedonia
in	India	zm	Zambia
kw	Kuwait	aw	Aruba
int	International Organizations	hn	Honduras
		fo	Faroe Islands
ve	Venezuela	py	Paraguay
yu	Yugoslavia	na	Namibia
lt	Lithuania	ad	Andorra
bm	Bermuda	jo	Jordan
cy	Cyprus	al	Albania
uy	Uruguay	uz	Uzbekistan
eg	Egypt	pr	Puerto Rico
ec	Ecuador	tt	Trinidad and Tobago
kz	Kazakhstan	gu	Guam
mt	Malta	ug	Uganda
ae	United Arab Emirates	np	Nepal
pk	Pakistan	gi	Gibraltar
lb	Lebanon	fj	Fiji
ma	Morocco	sz	Swaziland
ir	Iran	mu	Mauritius
ni	Nicaragua	sn	Senegal
sm	San Marino	zw	Zimbabwe
sa	Saudi Arabia	ai	Anguilla
bh	Bahrain	sv	El Salvador
lk	Sri Lanka	tn	Tunisia
pa	Panama	gb	United Kingdom
jp	Jamaica	dm	Dominica
bn	Brunei Darussalam	mz	Mozambique
ag	Antigua and Barbuda	mg	Madagascar
gt	Guatemala	lc	Saint Lucia
bs	Bahamas	nc	New Caledonia
bo	Bolivia	dz	Algeria
gl	Greenland	az	Azerbaijan
do	Dominican Republic	ky	Cayman Islands

Domain	Country	Domain	Country
vi	U.S. Virgin Islands	ao	Angola
md	Republic of Moldova	ws	Samoa
mn	Mongolia	vc	Saint Vincent an the
bb	Barbados		Grenadi
sb	Solomon Islands	tz	Tanzania
bz	Belize	tv	Tuvalu
vu	Vanuatu	sy	Syrian Arab Republic
bj	Benin	pg	Papua New Guinea
aq	Antarctica	pf	French Polynesia
qa	Qatar	om	Oman
gh	Ghana	ng	Nigeria
dj	Djibouti	nf	Norfolk Island
cf	Central African Republic	nato	nato
vn	Viet Nam	mr	Mauritania
cu	Cuba	ls	Lesotho
ci	Cote D'Ivoire	la	Lao People's Democratic
va	Vatican City State		Republic
to	Tonga	kn	Saint Kitts and Nevis
gy	Guyana	ki	Kiribati
sr	Suriname	kh	Cambodia
ne	Niger	gd	Grenada
gn	Guinea	fm	Micronesia
an	Netherlands Antilles	et	Ethiopia
ml	Mali	cm	Cameroon
ck	Cook Islands	bw	Botswana
bf	Burkina Faso		

Glossary

acceptable use policy (AUP) A set of guidelines that describe acceptable and unacceptable behavior when using the Internet.

acronym A shortened version of a word formed by the first letters of each word.

active link A hypertext link that is currently requesting information from the destination site.

archive A collection of files or artifacts.

ASCII text Conventional or plain text without any codes for special elements.

attachment A text file, image, sound, video, etc., that is included with an e-mail message.

author One who takes ideas and transforms them into a meaningful expression.

avatars Imaginary characters that you choose to represent you in a virtual reality environment.

bandwidth Space on a transmission line that affects the speed and the volume of information that can be sent.

bookmarks Electronic markers used to pinpoint a good site or important information.

browse To meander, to explore the virtual worlds of the Web.

browser A program that displays text and graphics gathered from the World Wide Web.

consortium An organization of entities united by common goals and concerns.

content site A Web site designed to offer ample, accurate, and appropriate information suited to the site's purpose.

context sensitive A software program that analyzes text for characteristics it recognizes; for example, the program may not operate if the wrong capitalization is used or the wrong sequence of commands is used.

counter A code added to the source code of an HTML document that adds to a visual display of numbers one time for each new visitor to the Web site.

cyberspace Descriptive term that applies to the world created by the computer in its memory.

dedicated search engine A search utility that uses all of its facilities to find information for Web users.

discussion list A list of members who communicate with one another through e-mail.

docuverse   A lending library; Ted Nelson's name for a digital library.

download   The process whereby a file on a Web site can be copied to an individual's computer or to a hard drive.

e-mail   Electronic mail; a quick message sent to someone else with an e-mail account.

e-mail address   Consists of an account name and a location where the person may be contacted.

flame   A sudden angry outcry or a stern correction for doing something wrong or saying something that is misunderstood or misinterpreted.

font   A distinctive typestyle.

ftp   File transfer protocol means that sites store software, text files, and some special use files that may be publicly or privately accessed.

gateway   A portal in a network that people can use to access a distant site or a local site.

gopher   A site or a hierarchical model of accessing information.

graphical user interface (GUI)   Displays text and graphics concealing programming code by using buttons to signify functions.

home page   Initial page in a series of Web pages.

hot buttons   When pressed, these buttons perform the preprogrammed function.

hot spots   Text, icons, or images that are linked to another document on the Web.

hypertext   Nonsequential text appearing as loosely linked fragments.

informational flow   A process by which information is passed on in a coherent pattern.

IRC   Internet relay chat uses channels to enable real-time messaging.

Internet components   Divisions of the Internet like ftp, gopher, WAIS, the Web.

Internet Protocol (IP)   An early method to follow to send packets via modem transfer.

knowledge tree   A hierarchical arrangement of information into major categories.

linear   Straight line; often refers to a mode of thinking or writing.

listserv   A discussion list in which all of the messages are automatically sent to all the members.

Memex   An imaginary machine that enabled its owner to keep up with scientific knowledge; from its concept we derive the theory of hypertext.

metasearch engine   A search utility that simultaneously examines several search engines to find a match to the user-defined search statement.

moderated list   A discussion group that has someone to read and approve messages before they are disseminated.

MUD, MOO, MUSH   Applications involving game playing and aliases in an IRC environment.

navigation   The active decision making to move through cyberspace.

network   An organization of computers, institutions, and people.

newbie   Someone who is new to Internet/Web exploration; a neophyte.

newsgroup   A discussion list with common concerns.

nonsequential   Out of sequence; nonlinear; random in nature.

object-oriented programming (OOP)   A concept of programming in which the program can act upon itself and in which the programming code is modularized. Objects can be created, passed, or called into other programs and can be imbued with behaviors.

packet   An electronic container that holds data and instructions on how to reassemble the data after it has been transferred.

path   A virtual roadway selected by the user.

promotional site   A Web site that may provide entertainment, games, rewards, and advisories about products and growth.

protocol   A system to govern the way information is accessed and transferred.

site owner   A person who has registered the domain name or has initiated the site as part of memory space leased from an Internet service provider.

smiley   A combination of ASCII characters to produce a visage like a smiling face; emoticon.

TCP/IP   Two protocols merged together as one; e-mail uses this protocol.

template   A reusable model in which new or changed information can be entered; templates in this book show a source code for a white paper, a resume, and a frame document.

transaction site   A Web site equipped with security options to allow Web users to purchase products, troubleshoot equipment, or gain technical support for systems.

UNIX   An operating system that enables computers to share information.

Uniform Resource Locator (URL)   The location of a Web site.

Virtual Reality Markup Language (VRML)   An open standard that uses HTML and three-dimensional modeling to create a fantasy world.

WAIS   Uses wide-area information servers to search through large networks and find information quickly; sometimes difficult to use; much of the same can be accomplished with search engines.

zine   An online magazine; an electronic periodical composed by individuals, institutions, and corporations.

Index